PENGUIN BOOKS
LET ME HIJACK YOUR MIND

Alyque Padamsee was a recipient of the Padma Shri, among India's highest national honours. Known as the Brandfather of Indian advertising, Padamsee headed Lintas in India and was responsible for some of India's most iconic ads, from Liril's 'girl in the waterfall' to Surf Excel's 'Lalitaji'. Besides his advertising accolades, he was a renowned theatre actor, director and producer, and directed seventy-seven theatre productions. He also experimented with more innovative productions that have made people rethink their ideas on modern living. He is the author of *A Double Life*, his memoir about theatre and advertising, published by Penguin.

Vandana Saxena Poria, the co-author of this book, is an OBE and among the top 100 UK–India influencers. She is known as the 'Human Alarm Clock' due to her disruptive thinking, which ignites people into action. She has lived across the world and built start-ups, selling one to a listed company. Gleaning insights as a chartered accountant and systems thinker, she links them together as a master storyteller to get people thinking differently. Vandana spent three years collaborating with Alyque on this book prior to his death.

T0154977

LET ME HIJACK YOUR MIND

MIND

ALYQUE PADAMSEE

with Vandana Saxena Poria

PENGUIN BOOKS

An imprint of Penguin Random House

PENGUIN BOOKS

USA | Canada | UK | Ireland | Australia
New Zealand | India | South Africa | China | Singapore

Penguin Books is part of the Penguin Random House group of companies
whose addresses can be found at global.penguinrandomhouse.com

Published by Penguin Random House India Pvt. Ltd
4th Floor, Capital Tower 1, MG Road,
Gurugram 122 002, Haryana, India

First published in Viking by Penguin Random House India 2022
Published in Penguin Books by Penguin Random House India 2024

ISBN 9780143466147

Typeset in Adobe Garamond Pro by Manipal Technologies Limited, Manipal

www.penguin.co.in

Dedicated to my favourite people
· The Youth of India ·

Contents

A Note from Alyque

As you have gone through life so far, have you sometimes found yourself stuck in a rut? Or have you ever felt like a hamster on a wheel, going round and round following the pressures of society and your peers?

At work, do you ever find your bosses or customers to be micro-managing and controlling? Do see people around you consistently looking to get one step ahead in the rat race of life? Do you ever feel constrained by this? Are you wondering if this is all life is about?

Then this is the book for you!

It all starts with your mind and these thoughts that you are having. Have you noticed that most people are thinking, and therefore living, with one foot in the past, regurgitating old, outdated ways of doing things?

My aim is to get people out of the stuffy thinking that is causing their brains to stagnate.

It is time to allow yourself to be HIJACKED and RESTART your thinking process. By getting you to question what exactly keeps you stuck in that rut or on that hamster wheel: the social norms that we have come to accept as gospel.

I am not saying what I've written in this book is the truth—it's my opinion. It's time you thought about why you follow the norms that you do.

This is a book designed to throw you all off balance in a good way, because it is crammed with ideas and fresh ways of thinking about how to live, how to dream and how to relook completely at your mindset and attitudes! As an advertising guru and thespian, my adventures in Idea-land have thrown up new concepts like the marriage licence . . . a fatwah against terrorists . . . bonus babies . . . and a myriad other concepts in revolutionary thinking.

My aim is for you to be stimulated. Throughout this book, I want you to shout out, 'Hey, I never looked at it like that!'

The aim of this book is to get your heart and mind reignited by blowing away all the norms that history is forcing on you along with the old ways of doing things. In this fast-moving environment, whether at work or at home, you need to be thinking differently and acting quickly to take advantage of opportunities. This book will give you the mental muscle to look at the world differently and, through the RESTART section, build the world that we deserve to live in instead of wallowing in the one we've got. At the same time, you will become leaders, creating a vibrant workplace that is future looking, despite the challenges that may come your way. This can only be done if mindsets change.

Through a new matrix I have invented—OICA (Observation, Insight, Concept, Actualization)—you can change negative thinking into positive action, and you can literally solve any problem by rephrasing the question! You will soon find yourself rejecting the most basic things that made you unhappy and coming up with new dynamic answers to questions like:

» Why inherit your father's religion?
» Why are multinational companies obsessed with GNP (gross national product) instead of GNH (gross national happiness)?

» Why should marriage be "til death do us part'?
» Why are terrorists breaking the law of their very own holy books?

The book interweaves insights from my life to help others question the unquestioned. I want to take you on a journey to understand that life is holistic and integrated in the same way that nature is. This book invites you to question the way you live your life and what you consider 'success'. Is life a wonderful gift which we have been misusing? Through my unique thought processes, I'm asserting that people are worshipping false gods (money, religion, marriage etc.). I want to plant different seeds in your head to get you to decondition yourself and create a new paradigm of living—one that is daringly different from old-world values:

» Lead a fuller life at work as well as at home—observing, feeling and learning all the time.
» Come up with new ideas and spot new opportunities.
» Be constantly engaged and involved! Take action where you are unhappy by recognizing what rules are making you unhappy.
» Build new value systems based on principles and proverbs that lead to greater understanding and collaboration.
» Grow business as nature grows: with violent happiness.

This book is a way to open windows in your mind, to think about life aside from greed, power and money. It is also a way to repay your fortunate accident of birth by helping the less fortunate.

It is ideal for anyone who is restless and believes there is more to life. For anyone in the process of building their career and wanting to bring innovation around them. And most of all for anyone who is determined to leave humanity in a better shape than what they were born into. As Einstein says, 'We cannot solve our problems with the same thinking we used when we created them.' So why not have fun discovering new ways of thinking the AP way?

Now tell me, are you ready to let me HIJACK YOUR MIND?

Introduction

Ronnie Screwvala

Co-founder, UpGrad; Founder, UTV Group

In this book, Alyque Padamsee is doing what he does best: provoke you.

In my opinion, Alyque Padamsee was one of India's greatest non-linear thinkers. The Brandfather of advertising and the father of theatre in India, Alyque's passing shook us all. Yet, few of us experienced the extent of another dimension of Alyque. And that is what this book is about.

Alyque was all about living with violent happiness, throughout his life, in whatever he did. You'll hear many from the theatre and business fraternity, including me, describe him as someone who always helped you maximize your potential and be your best. When people are at their best, Alyque says they become joyful, confident and curious. The result? It doesn't just improve life for them, it also improves life for everybody around them, creating happier societies.

But there's a huge part of the population that is not joyful. That are mentally still in chains. That believe they have to struggle with life and can't do anything about this.

Not one to allow this to happen, Alyque set out to create a guide for commandeering your mind and helping you realize what your own subconscious chains are.

What are those chains?

Through this book, Alyque delves deeply into entrenched social norms that most of us have subconsciously been hostage to and that bring unhappiness into our lives. He then turns our problems of unhappiness on their heads and forces us to examine their root causes again. He asks us whether it still needs to be like this or can we now give up these ghosts of the past that live on our shoulders, weighing us down? And he does this entertainingly, bringing in anecdotes from his incredible experience gained through seventy-seven theatre productions and over half a century in advertising, but also his long-lasting work through another side of his life.

Why does he feel the need to provoke?

India's secular fabric, composite culture, and pluralism were values that Alyque held dear. He felt that India (and the rest of the world) was a very unfair place, and many marginal voices have gone unheard due to the silence of those who did not speak up, that too for centuries. He was concerned about how religion was tearing apart the world, governments were not doing their job and the general brainwashing that went on in what is considered 'news'. He felt it was causing the vast majority of the population to feel trapped, be unhappy, doubt themselves and accept the situation like victims. But they weren't trapped, and he felt his last job on this planet was to provoke them into action. Because their lives and, more importantly, billions of other people's lives depended on it.

For decades, Alyque had worked relentlessly on improving society in whatever ways he could, be it working with the government during the 1992 Mumbai riots (at great risk to himself), or with Dalits on untouchability or supporting movements for justice and peace. His public service adverts were legendary, from tomatoes squashed in a jar to represent having too many kids, to coconuts being smashed to represent what happens if you don't wear a helmet. He was ingenious at creating and visualizing stories that haunted you and slowly changed your thinking.

This book is his final way of helping you change your thinking so you too can live with violent happiness and, at the same time, bring up those who are less fortunate than you.

There is no more important time than now to find a way to maximize the potential of everyone around us. With climate change and an increasingly VUCA[1] world, we need it more than ever!

But how exactly do we maximize this potential of everyone around us?

It all starts with your mindset—it is time to cast off those imaginary shackles of the past, to put those OLD ways of thinking to sleep, forever. It is time for you to question everything, from your religion to the way you work, the way you were educated or how you think about family and relationships. It is time to go against the tide on topics you feel strongly about, even though it's going to be hard. Remember, the wars of yesterday were won with bullets that killed. But the wars of today will only be won with bullets that disrupt the status quo. That disruption will start a chain reaction to bring greater happiness for you and all around you. And that's what Alyque is showing you in this book.

This is a book you can dip in and out of, again and again. It is going to stir up the opportunity to take a risk and talk about taboo topics like sex, extremism or death with your friends and family and blame it on Alyque—he would love that! You can have casual conversations with others on the questions he brings up. You can move the conversation forward. Most importantly, you can start to reform your own views on topics and norms that you have accepted as gospel truth. It is unlikely you will ever forget the marriage licence or look at arranged marriages in the same way again. When you next pick up a newspaper or go online to read the news, you will no doubt remember what he says about compartments in life. When you see a beggar on the street, you will realize you are a bonus baby. When you see an advert, you will wonder what part of you is being massaged. And you will question everything.

I hope *Let Me Hijack Your Mind* will inspire a new generation to speak up and change the thoughts around them to bring in greater equity for the billions who are in dire need of moving forward. Will you be that change agent that Alyque is looking for? You might just help change the world.

PART 1

HIJACK!

1

I Would Never Sleep with a Stranger . . . Unless It Was My Husband

AKA the Hypocrisy That Young India
Should Murder before It Murders Them

The Pre-ambling Ambling of AP: The State of Our Beloved Motherland

There's good news and bad news when it comes to Mother India. The good news is that India today, with more than a billion people, has 50 per cent of the population under the age of twenty-five. We are one of the youngest nations in the world!

What's the bad news? The bad news is that almost 50 per cent of our Parliamentarians are over the age of fifty-six.[1] Only 12 per cent are under forty and the average age is fifty-four. India's population is 48 per cent female, yet only 14 per cent of those governing the country are female.

So, tell me, if the country is being governed by a group of old fuddy-duddies who are mainly male, how do they cater to the needs of our 676 million younger people? You can see an obvious clash between old people and new ideas and young people and old ideas.

We know the only way to a healthy future is through progressive ideas. It is ideas that really change mankind. Since the beginning, when man realized how to make fire or invented the wheel, it was new ideas that transformed the world. Thank God for that first primate who had the idea of persistently walking on two legs, or where would we all be?

In our era, the most talked about ideas are to do with technology. When I talk about ideas, I am not talking about those types of ideas that make something faster or more efficient. I am talking about those ideas that change things fundamentally in the head. Ideas that completely change our way of thinking because those are the most powerful. Vandana reminds me that neuroscience, epigenetics[2] and studies around social norms[3] are helping us understand a lot more about why we think the way we do and why we hold on to regressive views and practices—it makes us feel safer; but it is the human brain and human attitudes that need to change if we are going to solve the major challenges that are impacting India. In short, *I believe we're over-conditioned! We accept everything that we've been taught as gospel, and worse still, taught NEVER to challenge anything. This is a disaster! For too long, our country has been following outdated practices because we have been continually worshipping false gods—gods that actually do nothing for us, and on the contrary, do lots for themselves.*

Time for a New Nation

I think a new nation should be created—I'm calling it Youngistan. And it is our best chance of saving ourselves from old, regressive thinking and to rid ourselves of the false gods, who should be shot to smithereens.

Youngistan? Where is that? Well, it is not a where: it is a WHO. Youngistan is all our younger generation of under-twenty-fives. They have the power to turn this country around, because I'm sorry to say, it's not going to be turned around by any of the political parties, that's for sure. The political parties have had long enough to prove that they can do it. It is time to anoint a new party and bring it to the table, giving our country the fighting chance that it deserves. The young generation will have to live with the choices being made now. But that will only happen if we can flush away the thinking that's left over from eras gone by. Unfortunately, these continue to be foisted on everyone in the country in the name of the sorry excuse of tradition and culture.

> *ALYQUEISM: It's time to decondition your brains, Youngistan, by swerving into the future, putting on a deconditioner and rethinking everything about our lives.*

Youngistan's Crucial Doctrine

It's time to decondition your brains, Youngistan, by swerving into the future and rethinking everything about your lives. And I believe that Youngistan's main job must be to *abolish hypocritical values*. This will lead to their heads being clearer and give them the ability to create a real space for new ideas based on new rules.

Let's look at where we need to swerve off the tried and tested path with old rules and apply a deconditioner to our minds. Here's a few to think about and discuss:

Sleeping with Strangers

For years, we have lived with hypocrisy and double standards. Here is a classic. I was at a club in Calcutta a few years back, giving a talk to a group of ladies there. They were all the well-to-do of the city, decked up in their fine make-up and drenched in jewellery.

I started with something they were least expecting. I asked, 'How many of you believe that it is OK to have sex with a stranger?'

They all looked at each other, shocked; a few even gasped and shook their heads in outrage. One lady raised her hand and said, 'Sir how can you say that? You are disgracing all of Indian womanhood! How can you say that? Sex with a stranger . . .' She turned her nose up and continued, 'Only those . . . American women you know . . . those people . . . the ones who end up divorced and all that . . .'

Later in the talk, I asked, 'How many of you ladies believe in arranged marriages?'

There was pin-drop silence as the penny dropped.

As they shifted about uncomfortably, I said to them, 'This is what you actually say to your kids—don't sleep with anyone before marriage, but marry whom I tell you, even if he is a stranger to you.'

Astonishing.

As you can imagine, these ladies did not take it sitting down—there was an uproar! They argued vociferously that it was 'different' and that I was taking the situation out of context. I on the other hand was astounded that the entire audience could not accept the fact that their daughters were sleeping with men they had hardly met until their *suhaag raat* (wedding night). You might not be surprised to know that I was politely asked NEVER to come back!

Look, I'm not advocating that we throw away all Indian values and start sleeping around with everyone. That is not my point. I am just saying that we should not have double standards. All across India, women are still forced to marry strangers. Other women (not the men, mind) are shunned by most of society because they have sex outside of or before marriage.

Youngistan, do you really want these double standards to continue?

Values: The Sins in English and Virtues in Hindi

It is a strange truth that hypocrisy is never seen in its true light, especially where language is concerned.

Let me give you an example. Is *nepotism* a virtue or a vice? It's a vice, right? We all agree that giving a job to one of your relatives out of turn is a vice. And yet, many of us, including me of the older generation, quite happily will react differently when we get a phone call from an uncle and he says, 'Beta, you know my grandson, *your* nephew . . . he's looking for a job in Lintas, you know . . . just accommodate him, huh?' And that is considered a virtue—to help members of your family to get out-of-turn jobs.

In fact, if you had said no to your uncle, he would have said, '*Arrey! Khandan mai parivaar ko naukri nahi dena hai, yeh kya baat hai?* Rishtedari *ka kya hua?* (Come on! Why would you not want to help out a family member? What happened to the importance of family relationships, to our *kinship*?)'

Therefore, when your uncle asks you to give a job to his grandson, out of turn, the pressure on you to comply is enormous. Or your uncle won't talk to you for the rest of his life.

And yet when we speak in English and use the word 'nepotism', it is a vice. When we speak in our native language ('rishtedari'), it suddenly becomes a virtue.

Let's think about old India and the word *rishwat*. Have any of you or your parents ever given rishwat? What is that? In the old times, the word 'rishwat' meant helping out others who were poorer; but let's be honest, look at the meaning that comes up when you type it into Google. 'Rishwat' is purely and simply *bribery*. Some of our older generation still believe that rishwat has to be given to get things done, and it is OK. Yet 'bribery' now sounds like a crime. In fact, in the UK and USA, it is now a crime for a company or any national of that country to give a bribe anywhere in the world!

Yet, we play with language so that it works in our favour. Think of this situation: so many companies now have a policy of 'refer a friend' for a job. And if your friend joins the company, then you get a bonus or a gift for introducing them. Yes, I'm scratching my head here. Isn't that the equivalent of a bribe? If not, why not? Surely we are just giving opportunities to those we know, who are likely to be of the same economic class and socio-economic status. It's actually a negative for those who don't have those connections.

So, tell me, what are the values that we're teaching our next generation? We say bribery is a terrible thing and yet we still bribe people left, right and centre! In some ways, we're just calling it a gift!

It's almost like having a table where bribery is on one side and a gift is on the other. Nepotism on one side, family and connections on the other. Can Youngistan alter this and bring about a much-needed change in our value system? Our value systems are completely corrupted, and it's in part because of language. We must get Youngistan to call out the hypocrisy of language and 'playing with language' to ensure that there are fair opportunities for all people, not just some people.

Youngistan, can you take this up on a war footing? Without this hypocrisy, aren't we going to be a stronger, better, happier nation?

Dis-crime-ination

OK, who believes in discrimination? I doubt any of you would admit to it. Discrimination, we all say, is a bad thing—many say it should be a crime! It is the white Americans who used to discriminate against the blacks (later, thanks to Trump, the Mexicans, too), and it is the Australians who have beaten up the Indians on the streets of Melbourne. And the rest of us get on our high horses, throwing our arms up in the air in despair.

Yet, around the world there are other forms of discrimination that are going undetected, or at least no newspaper/social media site is shouting out about them enough, which means nothing will happen about them, sadly.

For example, in India, in smaller cities and family businesses (less so in the MNCs now) what do we do? Vandana gives me an example—the situation is dire, though it seems amusing. She went for a meeting at a prestigious institute in Mumbai. The director there looked her up and down (she, as all women, is used to this) and looked at her business card.

He said, 'Where are you from?'

She answered, 'From London.'

He frowned, shook his head, and asked again, 'No no, but where are you REALLY from?'

She looked surprised and answered, 'Well my father is from Delhi and my mother is from Gorakhpur in UP.'

He tut-tutted and persisted, 'Saxena I understand of course, but this "Poria"—where is THAT from?'

She smiled at him, knowing what he wanted but determined not to give it to him. So said, 'From Rajkot, Gujarat.'

By now he was getting really annoyed. What he really wanted to know was her caste. He had never heard the name 'Poria' and therefore wanted to be able to put her into a box and label her accordingly. She was not having any of it. Needless to say, that meeting did not go too well for her!

You see, all across India, we still ask, 'Yes, but what caste are you?'

When we ask this question, we have automatically divided the country up into sections. Brahmins at the top, the Dalits at the bottom and in between we have so many. People react differently to you when you reveal your caste. If you are the same caste, then there seems to be a great kinship. What else is that if not discrimination? And the government has been trying (because of the Constitution) to restore justice by granting a certain number of seats in colleges and a certain number of jobs to the people who have been discriminated against for thousands of years.

OK, so perhaps it's not caste everywhere. Let's go deeper. There are countless stories from industry where people from tier 2 or 3 (smaller) cities are subtly discriminated against in the workplace by the people from tier 1 (metro) cities, because of their accent, their clothes, their language. They are laughed at and ridiculed by their tier 1 peers. Yet the bosses tend to turn a blind eye and put it down to youngsters having differences.

What about age discrimination? This whole business of older people finding it more and more difficult to find jobs is a classic example of discrimination. Surely even having a retirement age is a form of discrimination? Why should I have to retire because I have been around the sun a few more times than you? What about my knowledge and experience? If I can still do my job, why should I be forced out? Especially when people are living longer and longer? I will work until the moment my heart gives out. I could not sit still, knowing how much I could still give. Why should someone else take that opportunity away from me?

Isn't it time to make discrimination a crime, more so than just having government policies to avoid it?

So, you see again, it's all in the intricacies of making discrimination acceptable through language yet the substance of it being unacceptable in this day and age. *Youngistan, look through the language to see who is making a fool of whom, where hypocrisy is alive and kicking, then STOP IT from happening. Be careful when you are having conversations and question whether you are subliminally encouraging discrimination by answering a question like 'What's your caste?' or even 'Where are you from?' Ask yourself how that information is going to help you improve that person's life, not hurt it.*

The Country of WoMAN

Who reading this book believes in the suppression of women?

Are you mad Alyque, I hear you shout! This is the twenty-first century—equal rights and all that.

Let me show you the hypocrisy of the way we suppress women through tradition.

Discrimination of women—BAD.

BUT . . .

Pati Pooja (husband worship)? GOOD!

Dowry? GOOD!

In our country, discrimination against women is considered a fact of life. But the horror of it is that on celebratory days like Karva Chauth (do look it up if you are not familiar with it), many women are forced to say prayers for the long life of their husbands, who may have beaten them black and blue the day before. On this auspicious day, married women are supposed to fast from sunrise to the first sighting of the moon. They do this for the safety and longevity of their husbands. Do the husbands have to fast? Like hell they don't.

There are many such double standards. Do you realize that a woman has to BUY her husband in India? And I am not talking about the villages or the small towns, I am talking about my own city of Mumbai. I am ashamed. Every single city does this: 'Dowry *toh chal raha hai* (Dowry is part of the system).' You hear fathers saying, '*Arrey*, I must give my son a start in life. So, if *her* father wants to be so happy by giving him a nice Maruti . . . no not a Maruti, better he gives a BMW or something . . .'

We all tell lies—these are the double standards we have. Make no mistake, with a dowry, you are having your sons bought.

The burden on the bride's family is enormous. Isn't it enough that in the majority of cases, the bride has to leave her home and move in with the in-laws? That she must adopt the surname of the husband and cut her career short and bear children out of her body? That she has to look after the in-laws, often going without seeing her family for months? And on top of this, she has to PAY for the honour?

Youngistan, to have a truly equal India, can you throw these old traditions out? Can you say no to this type of treatment of women and create an equal place for all?

We Are Honourable Slaves

Look at the world. All around the world, we are taught to honour people around us. If they are older, or if they are a doctor, a teacher, a priest, a parent. Honour, honour, honour.

Let me tell you that honour in India is the biggest con. Like honouring your mother and father. What is the point of that? You only honour your mother and father if you believe they deserve that honour. But putting it down as a requirement that you *must* do this is totally wrong. I didn't honour my mother when I decided to marry Pearl, who was a divorcee with two children . . . In the old days, that was considered heretical. There is nothing heretical about that in today's age, everything has turned on its head and has a purpose . . . because I never looked at it that way. I fell in love with a girl, we separated for a while, and when she came back into my life, I was still in love with her. When I broached this topic with my parents, particularly my mother, she was horrified; she just could not accept it. And again, there are things like karma. My mother said, 'It's not in your karma.' I said, 'How can you know what my karma is?' Which also horrified her. She said, 'I know because I'm older than you and wiser than you.'

Thank goodness Priyanka Chopra's mother was more accepting when she brought home someone ten years younger than her. Now that's progress and good for them.

Vandana says that her children have taught her as much as her parents did. I too have learnt so much from my four children. So really, who should be honouring whom?

Here's a story which shows our wonderful side and also *how we are still slaves in our heads*. An American friend was in India for a year and travelled all over the country. At the end of his journey, he came and had dinner with me.

And I said, 'Joe, give me a one-line description of India.'

He said, 'One line? Impossible.'

I said, 'Please, an insight of some kind.'

He said, 'I'll tell you Alyque, wherever I travelled, I found the people of India were wonderful. They are hospitable, even if he's a farmer in a field and only sharing two rotis among his family. If I visit him at his home, he will tear one roti in half and give it to me. We all know that. Hospitality, generosity . . . *akalmand* [he had already learnt the word!] . . . very intelligent people and so on.'

He said, 'My one line would be, the Indian nation is a First World country. The Indian government is a Third World government. Why your wonderful people are allowing this to happen, when there's so many of you who could challenge it, is beyond me.'

And we continue to be slaves because we have been brought up *not to be demanding* and *to follow rules left, right and centre*.

Vandana's work concentrates on why our mindsets are the way they are and why we have an overdose of patriarchal, hierarchical thinking. From her research, the biggest problem that shows up is that from childhood we are subconsciously taught to obey rules without questioning them. So many people blame the education system for the lack of thinking ability, but she firmly believes it starts at home when you are not allowed to question anything and decisions are made for you instead of *by you*. As a result, you grow up to be people who are like robots, following a system, rather than individuals who are critical thinkers and have the guts to think afresh. For heaven's sake, how can you be, if you have never had the opportunity to question anything? Think about it. You have to ask your father for money to, I don't know . . . go out, buy anything, even go to college. They're always reluctant, unless it is about getting a good education so you can earn more. And our fathers are never questioned. What they DICTATE has to go in the house. Even when you're married and have children of your own!

The lack of thinking gets worse at school. Students tell Vandana all the time that teachers hate it when students disagree with them. And students are not allowed to question anything at most schools or higher education institutes. Which of you has ever had the nerve to ask a professor in college, 'Excuse me Sir, if you say India is a democracy, please tell us in what way?' But we don't. We never ask those questions in class, neither in school nor in college. And certainly, never at our workplace. I mean to go to the boss and say, 'I think the bathrooms in our office are terrible!' You'll find that you will have a demotion or a bye-bye letter on your desk within a day.

We are not used to demanding or being demanding, and it is time Youngistan began to exert those rights. India is a country which is taking its place in the world, on the world stage, in real terms: the economy. Unfortunately, on the social front, no, we are not. But I am sure that young India will be able to move us forward if they start working out what they should honour and what they should not. I am NOT saying be rude to parents or seniors. Far from it. I am just saying that be open-minded, that what they are saying may be in their best interest, as they understand it, but not in yours.

The Open Truth: We Are Slaves of the Media

There are people we can touch and see like our family and friends, and then there's a whole world outside that the media tells us about. We think we know them, even though we have never met them, whether it's Donald Trump or movie stars or people in your line of business that you've never met. And it is in that world that we begin to worship another set of false gods. We think of a model or actress, 'How fantastic, she's the most beautiful woman in the world.' But she is not. She is fed to us by the media. Just like these businesspeople who are anointed as hugely successful by the media powers that be. Not all of it is true: the media tends to build up myths about stars, giving people more due than their worth (or less, depending on who is greasing whose palms!). All movie stars have publicists, and businesspeople have their PR teams whose job it is to build them into a star and have *you*, the unsuspecting media consumer, following them wherever they go.

In addition to the traditional media, there is now also social media which is adding to the chaos. Its advent has no doubt created a more democratic medium, but some would say that there is too much choice out there now. But there are good things too—I'm quite surprised that my daughter Shazahn doesn't read a newspaper, nor my son Quasar either. He says all the news comes through apps on his phone. 'I get much more variety and I'm very happy with it,' he tells me. 'Now I can read whatever I want to read, from different places, rather than what one particular paper forces me to read.'

Whichever source it is from, many of us spend our lives talking about a vast number of people that we actually don't know personally but through our smartphones. And we read second-hand opinions of them from multiple sources to form our own (often entirely incorrect) opinion. We even talk to our friends as if we've been best friends with that celebrity because we think we know so much about them. They enter our life as uninvited guests, and before we know it, we become hooked on to a celebrity. If the celebrity is wearing the colour purple this year, we will subconsciously buy purple. Or buy the food they advertise. Or buy the car they drive. The media is good at getting you to give up two things: your mind-space (time) and your money!

Youngistan, it's time to think about how much time and money you can reclaim if you give up following people that the media want you to idolize. What about thinking about yourself and what you want instead of being slaves to media manipulation?

Youngistan—Stop Living by THEIR Values and Start Living by Your Own

This leads us to another hypocritical situation. Although the public media are gods, other media have given us alternatives. Nowadays, you can choose the media: the media doesn't choose you.

However, I've launched two newspapers in India, and it's clear that once people have subscribed, they generally don't change. If you have been with them more than six months, you will be with them for the rest of your life. So you then adopt the people they write about as your extended family.

I thought that social media would create a less conformist world, where you are then, in a sense, forced to think for yourself, which is good. However, we have the press relations officer of Donald Trump, saying, 'I have alternate facts.' Any sane person would say, 'Look, the facts are to the contrary.' Imagine him saying his inauguration was the biggest! No number of alternative facts proves this.

Donald Trump has learnt from Hitler. If you lie often enough, people will believe it. I saw with my own eyes Hillary Clinton becoming a liar and a crook. 'Crooked Hillary,' he called her. And every time the sub-heading would come on the news, 'Crooked Hillary'.

I said to people, including those in the media, 'That's not her name. He has called her that, but we should not.' However, the media began to be mesmerized by the label 'Crooked Hillary' (or the ratings they got from it), and eventually many people believed what was said, even though they did not know whether it was true.

Youngistan, will you hold the media to account and ask what values they hold themselves to? Will you shun them if they give you alternative facts and violate their values? Because if you don't, you can be sure that eventually your values will equate to theirs.

Fashion-able or 'Able to Fashion'?

Fashion, let me tell you, is one of the biggest cons in the world. There is a small crew of fashionistas who control the entire fashion industry, and because of that, the rest of the world is caught up in it. Fashion is dictated by this small coterie that tells you, 'Red is out this year and blue is in'.

Well I ask, who the bloody hell are they to tell me what to wear? It is like God speaking, or a commandment in the Bible, 'Thou shalt wear ultra-cropped tops of the purest white this season, or forever be ostracized.'

It's very lucrative, but honestly at another level it is nothing more than cheating. The whole industry is about leading the consumer by the nose, telling them what to think and then having the snooty ones turn their nose up at the ones who try to be individualistic. What happened to freedom? What happened to bell-bottoms? If you wore bell-bottoms today, people would snigger and ask what the hell you were wearing! Fashion should be individualistic and not mass dictated.

Fashion is like an infection. If you get infected, you have no option but to follow what the coterie demands. It becomes your 'fix', no different from that of a drug addict.

The cosy coterie that runs the fashion industry are false gods, built up by hype and the media. *But Youngistan, you don't need to believe that what they say about fashion is the gospel truth. You can create your own fashion and stop being a lamb who is gently being led to the bank account slaughter.*

Advertising

So we have to tackle advertising, which as you know was my bread and butter for many decades. Advertising is the home of emotional logic. A fantastic example is the longest-lasting slogan in the country for Amul's butter. Coined by Sylvester D'Cunha, it is 'Utterly Butterly'. What a catchy phrase, mainly because they've used the word 'butterly' deliberately. There's no such word: they made it up. But anyone one can tell you it means very tasty butter!

I say to you that emotional logic is a very powerful tool for advertisers.

Advertisers are often harmless—they're just hyping up the benefits. Usually they're not telling us false things, but just massaging the truth in a visionary way. Let's take the example of a project I did for MRF Tyres, who wanted an image for their tyres. In my research for doing an advert, we went to Koliwada, where truck drivers parked their trucks. We asked the truck drivers, who were mainly Punjabis, what they wanted most from a tyre. Without fail, almost all of them said, 'Tyre? *Majboot hona chaye.* (It must be strong).'

So I said, 'If they're looking for strength, the slogan should be MRF is the tyre with "muscle". Let's not say the *strongest* tyre—no one will believe it. If we say the "tyre with muscle", it means it's got a human value to it.' Everyone agreed.

I thought we should have a symbol, so we created the man holding the tyre above his head. The campaign was an instant success. Now that's emotional logic. It means the man is strong enough to hold a truck tyre above his head, which of course, is very heavy. It says nothing about the tyre. *It all works by association.* He's got muscles and the slogan is a tyre with muscle. And you build your own emotional logic that the tyre has muscle, even though that's not been said at all.

But things have changed in recent years. We now have movie stars endorsing products you know they don't use—our rational mind tells us this. For example, you know Amitabh

Bachchan doesn't eat Maggi noodles, or call Justdial. But people are subconsciously thinking, 'I like the association with a movie star that I love. I know it's not true, but I like the association.' A number of politicians like to have film stars in their election campaigns. It's a kind of rub-off impact, and next to cricketers, Bollywood tops here. So, this emotional logic is a manipulative logic and going back to the Amul example, nothing false is being said, because 'utterly butterly' is a tasty butter. They're just using suggestibility and hyperbole to say it's the tastiest butter. When you think of tasty, you think of Amul by association.

Why have I given you these examples? So you know what the industry is doing with emotional logic! And know where to draw the line.

Youngistan, I am asking you to judiciously think about what you see in advertisements because they can perpetuate myths that your mind can do without.

Conclusion

Time shall unfold what plighted cunning hides,
Who covers faults at last with shame derides.
                              —Cordelia, *King Lear*, Act 1, Scene I

I hope you have seen enough about hypocrisy in this chapter. Youngistan, I'm asking you to be that new generation that rethinks the values, rules and culture that are currently being followed in India.

I'm sorry, but my generation failed you.

It is Youngistan, the new generation who can think young, think new, think ideas, who need new values. They need to rethink those values that we are actually living as there's too much of a gap between what we speak and what we do.

But in true dramatic AP style, I insist that ideas are the only way to change India and bring us together. To be the One Nation that our forefathers dreamt of.

And what are the rare times we have seen One Nation? There are only two times in my life I have seen Indians become one nation. Not the usual, 'I am a Bengali' or 'I'm a Punjabi' and so on. Once when the Chinese invaded India in 1962—there were long queues at the recruiting office for the armed forces. It was wonderful, and it was fantastic to see that everyone was willing to defend our country. Of course, after that, we went back to our old ways.

Then in 2010 we had another very unifying factor when we all felt Indian—can you remember? It's the thing that seems to get us in the team India spirit. Yes, World Cup cricket unites us all.

But isn't it sad that we have this wonderful thing called 'India' but we are so divided? We are always ready to criticize the other party. So I say to you, if we want a united country, we've got to get rid of this discrimination against this, that and the other. Get rid of the hypocrisy. We have got to think as the Constitution says, 'every Indian will be born equal and will get equal opportunities'. That is the Constitution.

But the Constitution is a piece of paper, and how do you make a piece of paper like this stand up and walk and talk?

That's where Youngistan comes in.

Youngistan can turn pieces of paper into ACTION.

AND ACTION CHANGES THE WORLD.

Extracting the Essence

» 676 million young people are following the laws made by less than 1,000 old people in parliament.

» We need a new mindset to help these Youngistanis to succeed.

» Rooting out hypocrisy will give us space to think rationally.

» Subtle discrimination means unfairness to the people at the bottom of the pyramid.

❯❯ The Constitution is great in theory but people need to implement it fairly.

Hijacking Your Mind—Points for You to Ponder Over

❯❯ Which hypocrisies are you addicted to? Can you get rid of them?

❯❯ Which hypocrisies do you allow on your watch without speaking up?

❯❯ How can we bring in a fairer representation system for the people of India?

A Memorable Hijack

Raëll Padamsee

MD and CEO, Ace Productions and Numero Uno Productions, Founder and Managing Trustee, The Create Foundation

In 2021, the government took a step in the direction my dad pushed me into in 1980: reconsidering raising the marriageable age of girls in India. Dad made me promise him I would not get married until I was 30 and financially independent. All around me my friends from college were planning their Big Bash weddings, and here I was doing a part-time job, completing a Commerce degree and 16 different courses from interior décor to French so that I could get a well-rounded exposure to all that was available, and only then make my career choice. As per my Dad, theatre was definitely not one of them.

When I was 18, he bought me a car, got me to learn how to drive, be independent in short, and ensured that I was experienced enough to not feel dependent on anyone. A 21st-century Dad—hijacking my mind in the 1980s!!

2

A Union of Taxpayers
Who Refuse to Pay Tax

Brains Down the Drain

As I mentioned in the previous chapter, a few years ago, an American who came to India on a Fulbright scholarship who said, 'India is a First People nation with a Third World government.'

Think about it. We are a First World country with a Third World government that has let its people down since Independence. Now I know we are a huge country with a massive population, and it is not easy to govern here. But in this modern day and age, with artificial intelligence, real-time data and more, as well as the best brains on the planet for all things related to information technology, we *can* and should be governing better. But we are still in a sorry state, with no real accountability from the leaders.

For a lot of people, this hits the nail on the head, and it's worth reflecting on. Any Indian who goes to America does extremely well. The head of PepsiCo for many years was an Indian woman (Indra Nooyi); the head of Google is an Indian (Sundar Pichai); then there's Satya Nadella at Microsoft, and many more. Clearly, we have the brains. So, how did India become a Third World country then? The biggest challenge is that none of the top politicians of this country has ever run a company with governance. Running India is like running a multinational company, with all our states and territories.

You may be brilliant at the top, sending all the right messages, but it all depends on the people under you and ensuring governance down below in the organization. You see, in a company there is strict accountability enforced by the shareholders through third parties such as auditors. Auditors have a responsibility to the shareholders of the company, and they give their opinion on whether the business position shown by the directors is a fair reflection of what's going on in the company. Using specialized techniques, auditors will assess risky areas and examine documents. They then have conversations, and in short do what it takes to be sure that the financial statements are not misstated. They also put in place the checks and balances to ensure that no major fraud is taking place, customers are getting value for money and employees are satisfied. Fundamentally, they are checking that management are governing the company well and that value is being created. Vandana knows all about this as she was a chartered accountant in her previous avatar. Whether you're running a family business or a football team, whether you're operating a theatre or an arts association, their ability to keep going successfully has to do with governance and accountability at all levels. Governance is 'government' in the truest sense of the word. But what about our government? How accountable is our government? Who ensures accountability? And why can we not enforce it?

A Taxing Situation Made Untaxing

This was something on my mind for many years. I found out that years ago, Indian anti-corruption activist Anjali Damania had decided not to pay taxes until some accountability came into the government. They promised lots of things at the time of elections but what happened to those promises? I seem to recall the American Goldwater Institute in the USA also trying to file a case, but not as a union. It is time we all stood up!

I spoke to a lawyer in Mumbai. I said, 'We are consumers, you know. We pay taxes, like you go into a shop and you buy something. Let's suppose you buy a packet of Surf and you take it home and, in the box, there are stones. You'll take it back and you'll explain to the shopkeeper, who in turn will report it to Hindustan Lever. Hindustan Lever, I assure you, because I have worked with them, will send you two free packets.'

All of us who are working and earning have to pay tax. And we pay our taxes for what? Clean air, right? Good roads, right? Water supply, electricity, public transport etc. In short for all public services. But let me ask you, what are we truly getting in return?

I say we are being swindled.

So why shouldn't we have a taxpayer's union? If every factory can have a union, which protects the rights of its workers and ensures they have fair pay for their labour, why can't we have a taxpayer's union to ensure access to the right facilities?

This idea of a taxpayer's union is a serious thing. I don't want it to be another Lokpal Bill—you know, going on forever. We should be able to demand that we receive what is promised to us. At the moment, the challenge is that we are paying lakhs through taxes for the product, but we are not getting satisfactory quality. We are all taxpayers, believe you me, even the 80 per cent in the villages and small towns. Everyone is paying the Government of India tax, even if they are not earning directly. Remember, when they buy their bidis (local cigarettes), there's a value added tax. There is excise. There are all these invisible taxes that every single Indian amongst the 1.4 billion Indians that we have now (I wouldn't be surprised if by the time you finish this book it is 1.5!) are paying.

Wouldn't it be wonderful if all the taxpayers in this country said, 'OK, you either give us the value for our money or . . . we go on strike!' And certainly, some income taxpayers could do that very easily. And if the income taxpayers stop, this country would come to a standstill.

Do you know how many people pay income tax in this country? It is just above 1 per cent[1]! Those 1 per cent of people are the strongest force to demand a good product from the government. I genuinely believe that if you don't know how to govern, then GET OUT!

We do not need to make it a circus with a 'we will do this, and we will do that, and we will come out on the streets and we will demonstrate'. If we just stop paying our taxes, how will the government pay salaries then? That's what I'm advocating: a taxpayers' union.

In a corporate company, the shareholders have the right to question the directors who are making decisions for the company. In this situation, we the taxpayers would therefore have the right to question the government on how and where it is spending money.

I know it may sound ridiculous, but I have checked this out with lawyers. If there is a group of like-minded people who are part of the taxpaying population of this country, they can come together and form a union, the lawyers have said. And by law, a union is allowed to go on strike. We will strike by not paying tax.

What if we assembled a million people with a fee of one rupee each? What if we got senior lawyers on board? The main aim is not to show the government up, but to make the government accountable and actually get the services that have been promised to us, the people. The taxpayers' union would be totally legal, and we'd be covered by the union laws, so if the taxpayers go to the union and strike, we can bring the government to a standstill.

Come on! With today's IT infrastructure, isn't there a way of bringing in more transparency and accountability as well as democracy in decision-making? If we can bring in Aadhaar, surely we can build better systems that will ensure we are getting our money's worth as citizens. If we band together, we can force through changes like this.

ALYQUEISM: India is a First People nation, with a Third World government.

The Right to Recall

I understand that back in the early 2000s in California, USA, the people of the state felt their governor was not doing a good job. Remember, California has probably one of the most advanced kinds of government, where the people actually govern (!) as opposed to get their photos on hoardings and look for PR opportunities. If you collect signatures greater than 12 per cent of the number of votes cast in previous elections for that office, you can recall an elected official. Through various campaigns, they managed to get 18 per cent to sign the petitions. The guy lost his job. So in effect, it was the 'right to recall' a person if they are not performing.

That is what we need in India. Imagine an India where this was possible. It would lead us to being a First World nation with a First World government. Now isn't that worth unionizing for?

We must not make a scarecrow of the law,

setting it up to fear the birds of prey,

and let it keep one shape till custom make it their perch and not their terror.

Measure for Measure, Act II, Scene I

Extracting the Essence

» We have the brains to turn India around, but start with the layer below you.
» We should not be forced to pay for services we are not given.
» We should be able to vote out elected officials who do not do as they promised.

Hijacking Your Mind—Points for You to Ponder

» Whose brains are you not using in the workplace or at home? What if that person was the next Sundar Pichai or Indra Nooyi?
» What services have you settled for and why aren't you doing something about it?
» Who would complain about you and say you are not playing your role? What if you could be forced out over it? What would you do differently?

3

Do You Need a Licence to Marry Your Partner?

I've been married three times. And it's wonderful. Believe you me. I would do it three times again, there's no question about it! But unfortunately, with a marriage, people live under the same roof, share the same facilities, particularly the bathroom . . . well, that causes problems. If anyone wants their marriage to last, I suggest you build a second bathroom! People do not seem to like sharing bathrooms with anyone. Least of all their spouse or partner. Am I right?

As I've already said, the purpose of this book is to get people to stop believing in the myths and falsities of all this conditioned wisdom, conditioned reflexes to everything in life. We always seem to be at least a century or so behind in what we think are standard truths.

Well, a standard activity in the life of our species is that we fall in love. After a while (or much sooner in most cases!), we wind up having sex . . . and if the relationship continues, eventually the question of marriage comes up. It is often, especially in countries like India, considered an inevitability. But why? Are we confusing love, sex and marriage?

Let's look at these concepts of love, sex and then marriage.

ALYQUEISM: Is marriage 'til death do us part or 'til death do us boredom?

Love

Love, love, love. The word is so overused. I love you, but mind you, I also love my car. And of course, I love Baskin Robbins ice cream! We use this word interchangeably in so many different ways that we completely dilute its meaning.

While I could quite possibly write a book on 'love', what with my love of theatre, my love of advertising and my well-known love life (!), I wanted to explore the idea of love between beings of our species: humans. Speaking to many different people over the years, I see where the problem lies. You see, what we watch in the movies is *not* what happens in real life. This whole 'I met someone and he or she swept me off my feet, and now we will live happily ever after' does not exist; yet it is continuously rammed down our throats. And yet generations still think it does exist.

So I decided to examine this thing called 'love' in one of my last plays, called *Legend of Lovers*, in which my daughter Shazahn played the lead. The playwright starts with the old idea of love, very poetic, and we show this with the couple dancing together, dewy-eyed, saying clichéd things to each other. But that's a love that will never last. I mean really, is there such a thing as everlasting love? Poets say it, as do songwriters, 'I will love you to the end of time', and it's very easy to say to the one we love.

I say, how stupid.

The play goes on to show the characters depict this change and this eternal love morphing into other things, until perhaps it is not love anymore.

In the real world, love seems to be all about expectations these days. If you love me, you'll behave in a certain way. And if you stop behaving in that certain way, I might stop loving you, because you no longer fulfil my expectations.

Love changes as you change. And we keep looking for that everlasting love that can't exist as we would have to stand still. Don't forget, so would that other person in order for it to be everlasting and *exactly the same* love.

Sex

Most of the time, people don't fall in love anyway. It's not falling in love—it's falling in body. They fall for chemistry. We see this in nature: nature dictates that there should be a relationship between a man and a woman, so they can procreate. That's the same as all of nature and the animal kingdom. You see this on those marvellous documentaries on National Geographic, which show the whole life cycle. Animals choose to mate, and some will go on to look after the child together, at least for a while. Once the child has grown somewhat, most animals often seek other mates. I say that is what nature intended for humans too—after all, we are animals just like the rest. Nature didn't intend 'til death do us part' because that's a ridiculous idea: you will get bored out of your mind.

But people often mistake the chemistry of wanting sex for love. Sex therefore is purely a body love of the chemistry between the people. It is an aphrodisiac. But your body chemistry has nothing to do with love. It is very deceptive. We fall in love with body chemistry for a very good reason: to propagate the species. Nature designed it, not us. Advertising and media have done a bloody good job of augmenting it, though.

The love we feel for another human being is not blind, as the expression goes. Love is invented most of the times.

By whom?

By you.

Years ago, I thought I was in in love with a girl. I told one of my very close friends, 'I think I am in love.'

He said, 'What do you like about her, besides looks and all that? What else do you like?'

I said, 'She has a great sense of humour.'

'Give me an example.'

I thought and said, 'The other day we were together with some friends and I was cracking a few jokes. She was the one that laughed the most.'

He said, 'That's not a sense of humour. She was laughing at your jokes. So, she has a sense of fun, she made an effort to understand *your* humour. A *real* sense of humour is when you can laugh at yourself.'

I realized what he meant.

I said, 'You're damn right. I invented the idea that she has a great sense of humour because I wanted her to be the girl I was in love with. I didn't see *her* sense of humour. And I invented many other things about her to convince myself that this was love.'

That's not real love. I think sometimes we get mixed up. I think the traditional notion of love, that people actually yearn for, is about cherishing someone. If you love someone, you cherish them. You want to protect, support and care for that person, no matter what happens. It is not a tap that you turn on and off depending on whether the other person meets your expectations, or vice versa. And sexual love does not necessarily signify cherishing. A person who cherishes the other person will go all the way for that other person. Do you have that in your life? Or do you consume love, like just another snack that will fill you up for a little while, then leave you with a void?

Regardless of how you view love, especially in this day and age, I do want to ask you, what does cherishing and love have to do with this age-old concept called marriage?

Conventional Wisdom Belongs in the Convent

Here's one convention. Conventional wisdom is that marriage is religious practice. In the Christian sense (and most of the other ones as well, although they don't say it in so many words), marriage is forever. That beleaguered expression "til death do us part' is taken as a standard of a good marriage.

I think a good marriage is something that gives joy to both parties, and as long as that joy is there, they feel like they have a good marriage. Then at some point, for some reason or the other, they lose that joy. And then they really have a bad marriage which they struggle on with. Just like my parents, who had a bad marriage . . . Do you know that my mother never spoke to my father for over forty years? This is the kind of thing that we blindly believe in.

The idea that you and I must be a thing that lasts forever has been a burden on the vast majority of us and has come from religions. The Christian religion says it in black and white:

'When a woman marries, the law binds her to her husband *as long as he is alive*. But *if he dies*, the laws of marriage no longer apply to her.'[1]

And, 'A wife is bound to her husband as long as he lives.'[2]

Goodness! Look at the misogyny of the phrasing, let alone the issue of being bound for life. Women have been getting a raw deal for a long time, but we will discuss that in the next chapter.

As Vandana reminds me, 'If you think of when marriage started [thousands of years ago], you probably only lived to be thirty. So, you were really only married for fifteen years. But now you get married in your twenties and you're expected to be with that same person until you're eighty-five . . .'

'Til Death Do Us Change

I think in the past, being together until death gave a permanence to society, because if you had people disengaging from marriage and not accepting responsibility for the children, it would have been very difficult. In the old days, women didn't work, so they were not money earners. It kept the men in line. And the law of the past said, 'You're the male. Even if you want to live separately, you have to give a maintenance allowance to the wife and kids.' That was considered acceptable and necessary, but it was still rare for this to happen. But once women became more equal, got jobs and became more independent, things changed. We started to see that if the male was unhappy and wanted to depart, they should be allowed to depart. Equally, if she was unhappy, she would depart. Or in many cases, they just didn't want to be married any longer, where the marriage outlasted its joyfulness.

We also now see another myth gallop onto the scene—along with marriages MUST last forever, we were told that they were only for a man and a woman. But nothing is certain, everything changes. Now we see gay marriages. Women's rights have come in. Child laws have been established. Society is changing, but in the area of marriage, which impacts 70 or 80 per cent of the world, there are no changes. Yes, there's divorce, but divorce is always messy. There's always wrangling, and there's emotional disquiet, especially with children.

This has led me over the years to wonder if it is time to rethink this cliché 'til death do us part'. Does it lead us eventually to boredom and divorce?

I have a solution that is simple and practical but outrageous.

Most activities that require a level of proficiency require evaluation and licences. Think about it—at school, you're evaluated at the end of each year. It is the same in college. Even when you go to work you have a year-end appraisal. But when do you review your marriage? I have talked to hundreds of people, and many of them (especially the women) have loved this thought . . .

A Five-Year Marriage Licence

'That's absurd!' I hear you say. Well, all new ideas sound absurd at first.

Hear me out, because this absurd idea will save marriages. Not once in my three marriages did I sit down and assess whether I was a good husband. Nor did my wife sit down and ask whether she was a good wife. You might treat your wife badly or she might treat you badly. And that kind of taking for granted is what ruins one of the finest institutions in the world: marriage.

So in the fourth year of the marriage licence (which might expire next year because it will be the fifth year), you'll suddenly say, 'Hey I don't really want to lose my wife. She's a wonderful person. I really haven't done much. We haven't been to a movie for about two years together. We haven't been on a holiday because I've been so busy . . . I very rarely take care of the children; she does all that.'

You begin to reassess yourself, and the wife says, 'I used to work as well as make time to cook for him and the family and now I don't. I've been too busy!' What I'm saying is, it's a corrective measure. It's an opportunity for both parties to assess whether the marriage is working. Imagine if one of the parties, say the wife, says, 'It is not working!' And the husband thinks, 'Yes, it is working, and I don't want to lose her.' He suddenly will become the boyfriend who woos her before the licence expires. But currently, there's is no assessment at all, and the relationship is not evaluated emotionally.

Such a licence would avoid the acrimony when you go into the divorce court. Oh, haven't I seen it enough! You meet two people who have been sharing their lives, their bed, their children, and suddenly they've become tigers: 'GRRRRRR, I must have the car.' 'No, you won't have the car!' Wrangling over the children and what used to be a wonderful relationship suddenly comes down to a bare-knuckled fight. Let me tell you for those who are contemplating a divorce—if you are in California, whatever you have is divided fifty-fifty regardless![3] Yet elsewhere, the whole process becomes very costly. The divorce lawyers in Mumbai (who I may have some experience of!) charge astronomical sums just to work out all that. And at that point you have no option, because nobody in your family is talking to anyone in her family, so you have to get a lawyer.

So, how would the five-year marriage licence work in practice?

A lawyer draws up a marriage licence, which stipulates that the marriage will be automatically dissolved in five years if either party does not want to continue. This licence is preceded by a prenuptial agreement, detailing the sharing of wealth, children and other important elements, in the event of the licence lapsing. If the couple wants to continue being married, they can renew their marriage licence but only as long as both agree. And four years later, the wife and the husband both get a chance to re-evaluate their relationship.

So, there would probably be a huge supply of marriage counsellors to deal with situations where only one party wants to renew the licence. Can you imagine what they would say? 'I know you are not getting on. But remember, she won't be there when you come home. Same with her, he won't be there. Children will have to split their time between the two of you. Is that what you want?' And then it becomes a discussion point.

Why can't we just have a marriage licence starting with a validity of five years? And if you want to continue at the end of five years, you renew your licence just like the driving licence. I do believe it will make happier marriages and result in fewer cases of divorce, because at the end of the period of five years people will come to know the other person reasonably well. And they may say, 'Well I don't want to live with them anymore', or they might say, 'I'm going to lose the person who really understands me. I realize that now'. The sense of loss only hits home when the ugly word 'divorce' enters the picture. One or both just do not understand each other and therefore have to go through a divorce.

If you come to a dead end in a marriage and you go on living in a dead end, then you are not really living. I'm saying I'm abolishing divorce . . . you sign an agreement, and at the end of it, there's no messy divorce, just a contract.

But anyway, a five-year marriage licence is, I feel, around the corner. If it doesn't appear in India first, that's sad, but it will come into law somewhere. And I think it will probably be in Sweden, where the people are quite advanced in such matters compared to everyone else in the world.

> For what is wedlock forced but a hell,
> An age of discord and continual strife?
> Whereas the contrary bringeth bliss,
> And is a pattern of celestial peace
>
> Henry VI, Act V, Scene V

Postscripts

Why Five?

People have asked me why I said a five-year marriage licence and not seven or ten. I had originally thought of *The Seven Year Itch*, so I said seven years. People said, 'Are you crazy! It is horrible much before that!' Well, most men tell me that they are getting bored after five years. Most women tell me that they are taken for granted after three years, and at five they are done. So, I settled on five.

Postscript 2: Women—Stop Being Hostages!

Because women were brought up to nurture others, marriage became part of life. In fact, the most important part of life for a woman in India and to a lesser extent in the West is having a husband and a marital home; these are considered part of a woman's DNA. She has been taught to believe this, BUT IT'S NOT TRUE! A lot of American women are leaving their husbands and their children and just vanishing. Have you seen the brilliantly conceived movie

Thelma and Louise? The two women decide, 'Let's go on holiday together, and not tell our husbands; let's disappear and see what comes next.' Well, that is happening in real life.

A woman in India has to realize that she can go too. As women have gained equality around the globe, we have seen differing trends. There's an increase in the number of divorces, leading to many divorced women happily living alone. Another group of divorced women are also very happy living with others. Another group of women who don't want the children tell the husband, 'You take the children.' Fine.

Women, I am hijacking you. I am asking you not to be hostages of old tradition. Do what works for you. If you are happy, all around you will be happy.

The New Joint Family

I was talking to a friend about joint families, and I said, 'I've got a joint family.'

He said, 'What rubbish! Joint families are old-fashioned; you're modern.'

I said 'My three ex-wives, my children and I celebrate each other's birthdays by having a party. That's a joint family. We're separated through divorce but we're there emotionally and in spirit.'

He thought it was very funny and very cute. And that led me to think that there would be much less tension and meanness in the world if divorced couples were friends. Parting amicably. I find that divorced couples rarely speak to each other again because they've said such slanderous things about each other in court.

'That sounds all very well in theory, but how do you do it in practice?' Vandana asks me.

I tell her that I have tried to keep a friendly relationship with my ex-wives and a very strong bond with each of my children. It led to a minor miracle, which happened when my third child, Shazahn was three years old. My first wife Pearl wanted Shazahn to be baptized. I asked her why. Pearl said that she wanted to be Shazahn's godmother! Goodwill knows no boundaries.

Another time, Pearl was sick with a heart problem. I said to Dolly, 'Let's get presents. And let's go to Pearl's house. We are all a family. We're divorced but it's only on paper. We're still a family.'

And from that day onwards. Dolly and Pearl began to talk to each other. Then later Pearl talked to Sharon, who by the way was one of her actresses. Everyone talks to each other, sends WhatsApp messages, and we are together for my birthday every year. We have removed that hate; the edge has been blunted. Honestly, I'm not sure whether they love it. But it's the new joint family.

'What's the impact now?' asks Vandana.

Well, when Quasar now has a problem, he goes to see Sharon. And when she has a problem, she rings Q. And Shazahn and Q are the greatest of buddies. We went to Raell's house for an India–Pakistan cricket match—she invited Quasar, Shazahn and me. We all sat in the drawing room. She put up a big TV screen and we all watched India being beaten by Pakistan. And they were laughing and joking together. I said 'Wait a minute, who is that boy? Oh, it's my second wife's son, and that's my first wife's daughter, ALL laughing and joking together.'

That's how it should be. We have to break some of these old ideas. Human relationships cannot be ruled by tradition.

I read a lovely piece by Q. It's an old piece about family and he talks about when Shazahn was born. He said it was the time when the family, really for him, came together. I personally credit Sharon for bringing us all together.

Marriage IS wonderful while it lasts, but if you get divorced, don't hate the other person. You have a relationship with that person. They must have meant something to you. You just can't hate them.

So create your own new joint family.

It's a (Joint) Family Affair . . .

So, how did we manage to keep it all together, between three ex-wives and the kids? Let's hear from them.

'Remember when you're a kid, every fairy story you're reading is about the wicked stepmother and how badly she treats the step-child,' Quasar says. 'Think of Sleeping Beauty, Hansel and Gretel or Cinderella . . . it's just perpetuated that the stepmother is going to be evil. Whether you like it or not, those kinds of thoughts cross your head as a kid. So, when I heard about Sharon, I thought I was doomed. But Sharon was as far as you can imagine from those stepmothers. She really cared for us, and she also had a brilliant way of making us feel needed. She would call me up when it was coming up to Shazahn's birthday and tell me I simply *had* to be there to help out and babysit. I felt great about being asked to be there.'

Sharon has a no-nonsense attitude. 'Most barriers are man-made,' she says. 'And if they can be made, they can be unmade. We tend to make judgements about people before we have even met them, especially where broken relationships are involved. Raell and Q were just kids and they didn't need to be overloaded with stuff their young minds were unable to process. Having come from a separated family, I was determined that I would do whatever was in my power to remove any of those barriers.'

This certainly continued successfully. Shazahn adds, 'I was the youngest, and for me the cool thing was that I didn't even know what a half-brother or half-sister was until I was around thirteen. So, I didn't have any sort of preconceived notions about it, which I think, in a way, was a blessing in disguise. And I always treated them like my own brother and sister. I think at some point I even asked Dad, "But if they're my own brother and sister, why don't we live together?" He told me they were focused on their careers and that's what I should think about too.'

Raell agrees with the others and also credits other members of the family. 'Jerry and Rosh (Alyque's siblings) were very instrumental in influencing Dad that the family unit is very important and you have to mend bridges. He took that to heart and always ensured he had a distinctive relationship with each one of us independently. He also was quite adamant that on his birthday, he only wanted us there, despite having so many close friends and extended family. That cemented us all as a unit.'

It's a joint responsibility to create a joint family.

Extracting the Essence

» The word love is overused and has become meaningless. Real love does not stand still.
» Sex is bodily chemistry and unrelated to love.
» Marriages were invented in a time where it was a necessity.
» If we have licences for everything else, why not marriage?
» Don't allow long-standing traditions in the world to make you a hostage of your mind. Your traditions don't OWN you.

Hijacking Your Mind—Points for You to Ponder

» What is 'real' love to you? Honestly?
» Are sex and love the same thing for you? If so, why?
» In this day and age, is the traditional concept of marriage still relevant for you, and if so, why? Do you want someone to love you or are you looking for something else?
» Have you reviewed your marriage or relationship lately? What score did you give yourself and what can you do to better it?

4

Ten for Men
(and Zero for Everyone Else)

Patriarchy or Patri-history?

It's a funny old world we live in. We acknowledge that women are 48.1 per cent of the Indian population. While 1.9 per cent less than parity might not sound a massive difference, it means there are 54 million fewer women in India than men. Incredible. If you trawl the internet, there are countless articles about villages where no girls are being born to villages where there are no women to marry. 'Tut tut,' I hear you say. 'But Alyque, it's the problem of backward rural India.'

I'm afraid not.

Let's come to the issues facing urban India. While the sex ratio in our capital is around 866 female babies to 1,000 male babies, you might be surprised to know that some of the most affluent areas of Delhi have the lowest ratio—around 775 females to every 1,000 males born. I hope you are raising your eyebrows. Now think about the fact that while over 50 per cent of people graduating with a bachelor's or master's degree are women,[1] women account for *only* 10.3 per cent[2] of the urban labour force in India. Many firms are proudly saying that 50 per cent of their new hires are female, but this decreases drastically the further up in an organization you go, where differing reports say women hold between 4 and 36 per cent of senior management positions.[3] And only 2.8 per cent of Indian companies have female-majority ownership.

So, what is going wrong?

Everything in our world today, in my not-so-humble opinion, is judged by men's standards. And therefore, women don't have a hope in hell.

Why? Just look at what men's standards seemed to be based on, according to the state of the world, the world wars that have taken place and extremist activities.

Aggression, power and money. Their idea of beauty, their idea of progress. It is no wonder we have ended up with the world we have got. Whether you look at consumerism or capitalism, it is all built on the hallmarks of dominance—no matter what, beat the others to find your place at the top. Be lauded in the press, have the most employees, most offices, make the most money (although let's turn a blind eye to how you did it), be the toughest, maim your competitors and take the biggest risks. I'll say it again: the prevalent culture pretty much all round the world is one based on the triad of aggression, power and money. And a part of this is very firmly keeping women in 'their place'.

This triad seems to have been a dominant ideology within patriarchy for millennia. Vandana brought up an interesting point the day we met. 'In this world, for good and for bad, 80 per cent of history has been written by men and about men, 80 per cent of religion has been written by men about men, and 80 per cent of arts and literature has been written by men, for men.'

Without blinking, I said, '80 per cent! It's much higher than that, don't you think?'

'I know that,' she laughed, 'But at least nobody disputes that 80 per cent. If I had said 95 per cent, I would get people saying,

"But what about her and her? They've contributed." This way, I get people to think about the fact that despite 50 per cent of this world being female, the decisions of power and control have been decided by the other 50 per cent. What if this wasn't so? How different would the world be?'

Since the late 1700s with Mary Wollstonecraft in the UK, the feminist movement has been marching forward in stops and starts. It gathered pace in the 1800s with the pursuit of legal rights for women, especially when it came to education and paid work. And of course, in the early 1900s we had the suffragettes fighting for a woman's right to vote through various means, including chaining themselves to the railings of the Prime Minister's residence in London. But do you realize that women only got the right to vote in most of the world a hundred years ago? So for most of humanity's existence, 50 per cent of the population had little or no say in the governing principles on how humanity should live.

I think that the Second World War was really the time where women were given an opportunity to do everything, from making clothes to machines, as the men were off on the front line. But of course, when the men came home after the war, it petered out, and women were left with a taste of what they were capable of, but did not necessarily have the means to show it. The number of years it is taking to get to parity is quite incredible.

So, female emancipation is taking an exceedingly long time in many areas. For example, while the West has had its sexual revolution, I'm afraid we in India have been stuck fighting battles with poverty, domestic violence, marriage rights, property rights and others. Sex was left languishing in the closet and never given an airing. Even in the 1990s, when the LGBTQ movement took off in the West, that's when the closet was opened here ever so slightly. So now there are conversations around AIDS, LGBTQ and sex work. But we have to understand, for the longest time, dominant female conversations were not happening (which is why we need unspoken dialogues—see Chapter 11). And so, in a sense, women in India still do not own their sexuality. That's something that needs to change because without that, they will never be truly equal.

Make no mistake—as a result, patriarchy has consciously and subconsciously been alive and kicking for years in India, dominating every aspect of our lives. It's about time we realized that gender is a social construct and that patriarchy has been using this to its advantage, certainly for the better part of the last 2,000 years.

---

*ALYQUEISM: Patriarchy needs to fall off centre stage. Women, the floor is yours. **IF** you are willing to take it.*

The Less Considered Victims of Patriarchy

We all know that women have had it rough, but what about the men? I would assert that many men have become victims of patriarchy, almost as much as women.

How so?

Well, let's start with one of the age-old challenges of men. 'I can't help it—it's the testosterone in me that makes me sexually virile and this aggressive.'

In patriarchal cultures, we have been told, testosterone is definitely one of the key drivers. This critical hormone has done us well for many millennia—it certainly helped cavemen kill animals to feed their family as well as deal with other threats in their daily lives. Recent studies show, I'm told, that testosterone levels go up during aggressive behaviour in sports, as well as in prisoners who have committed violent crimes.

The outcome?

Because of the subjugation of women and the supremacy of the male, certain unwritten rules have become the social norm.

Like men staring at women's breasts.

Let's face it, many women are attractive, and many males still believe it is their right to stare or even approach women with the thought that something physical could happen between them (regardless of how the woman thinks). Indian movies have long depicted this: how many movies have shown the butch hero not giving up on the heroine, despite her non-interest, with the heroine eventually falling into his arms? In the West such behaviour would be considered stalking, but in India, it has been the norm ever since movies were invented. It's something that is hardly talked about and that often gets swept under the carpet, along with a lot of misogyny.

Imagine for a minute the millions of poor, uneducated youths who watch these movies. Without role models telling them it is wrong, they become self-styled Romeo stalkers causing untold harassment to women. And who is there to tell them this is wrong? In the past, NO ONE. In fact, the older men would often wink them on. Unfortunately, it is not just the movies showing us bad behaviour. In the real world, let's not forget how many men have gotten away with raping women, because it is always the man's word against the woman. This is particularly the case when there is a hierarchy based on caste. She is silenced in shame and law, because either no one will believe her or will tell her it was her fault.[4] The men believe it is their right, often telling themselves and others that they have uncontrollable urges to satisfy and that's what women are there for.

But hold on a minute. Is that uncontrollable urge because of testosterone or because of culture? If you go to a nudist beach, it is unlikely you will see loads of men staring at naked women and not able to control themselves—it just doesn't happen. And there are countless indigenous tribes all around the world that prefer to be naked, and they don't get aroused 24/7, 365 days a year. See, the discussion is not about biology—it is not because of testosterone that we have these social norms. It is because of culture. A culture that gives one gender power over another. A culture that serves men and sees women as a prize or possession.

Times change. In fact, sometimes the past is way ahead of where we are today. During the Renaissance and the nineteenth century, the female breast was considered a thing of beauty, and women used to wear gowns that revealed their breasts. I remember this very clearly in the stunning costumes of the sixteenth century. That didn't mean that any man could go fondling the breast of a woman. He could remark on the beauty of her breasts just as he could talk about the beauty of her eyes. However, everything changed again with the prudes over in Victorian England, who unfortunately brought those views over to India. It also became the norm over here.

But while the West moved on from those regressive views, we in India did not.

The result is that in India today, even as we pretend to be prudish, we are nothing of the sort underneath. Think about the saree—it's about the most sexy, shape-showing outfit you could wear, accentuating the cleavage, bust and butt. We have also hung onto the acceptability of the lecherous eye, which has caused (and continues to cause) a lot of damage over the years.

That age-old misogyny is being challenged through #metoo and more open dialogues in the twenty-first century. After 2,000 years (maybe more), suddenly, women are starting to speak up in a bolder voice and in larger numbers.

The result is many men are starting to reassess their position. For years they have been forced to follow social constructs of what a 'real man' is—expectations of being the breadwinner and head of the family, that boys don't cry, that they are supposed to be strong. There is a huge burden on them as well. What about men who want to share the burden of household chores? They are often ridiculed by their friends for being hen-pecked. What about men who don't want to work? Or want to depend on women financially? Not being able to live, their free will has caged them too. It is a burden that both genders have been shouldering for too long.

The 'Old' Still Screws the 'New'

How are men reacting?

Depending on their upbringing, not well. We can see that men are not very welcoming of women into 'their' domains, because most global organizations, whether public or private, are still full of old, white males—remember the small number of women in senior management. This number is increasing, but it is still at a pathetic proportion to the old men. Patriarchy at its finest! How does that compare to the population, especially when it comes to male–female ratios? So, if men were really so equality-minded, why would this still be the case?

Get ready for something in true AP style: I think the real reason women are not making it to the top is that men fear women's potential, they fear not being in control. Why else would men fight so hard against it? Are men frightened that women can beat them in intellectual and physical prowess?

To examine two distinctly separate fields, look at sports and board exams globally . . . Females are starting to outstrip males; it is a trend. Finally, women seem to be on the road to finding their equal, rightful position in society. But many members of both sexes are not happy about it. We have seen many Trump supporters in small towns, where the wives themselves are saying that they just want to stay at home, look after the kids and be looked after by their husbands. They don't aspire to anything. And then, of course, we have the men who are keeping women down by not promoting them, as they do not have the 'right' experience or attitude. To what? Be patriarchal?

Even books and movies are changing, but again, only recently so. Vandana reminds me of the Bechdel test,[5] the famous check of whether there is gender equality in fiction or a movie where they ask three questions:

1. Are there more than two female characters?
2. Do those two females talk to each other?
3. Do they talk about anything other than men?

Surprisingly even in 2018, only around 50 per cent of fiction and films passed this test. But the number is growing.

There are a few old esoteric spots where the 'old' maintain their muscle power, those continuing male bastions that keep the male pride alive. For example, the largest prize money for all major sporting competitions goes to male competitors. However, the 'new' are encouraging sports for women to great results. We've now had the best female under-19 cricket team. Women's soccer in the USA is watched more than its male equivalent. But it is going to take something really big to knock men off their patriarchal pedestal, in favour of women even getting a step up in all areas they should.

And that means taking males down a peg or two for behaviour that is simply unacceptable in today's day and age.

Time to Pester the Molester

With the knowledge and culture we have easily available today, it is distressing to read that women on the streets all around the world are being molested daily. Even in Mumbai, of all places!

The shocking Shakti Mills gang rape[6] in Mumbai in 2013 shook a lot of women. A twenty-two-year-old photojournalist was gang-raped by five men, including two minors in the Mills compound, where she had gone with a male colleague. They tied him up and raped her six times, holding a beer bottle to her neck to stop her from screaming. In a bid to keep her quiet, she was told if she went to the police, they would post naked pictures of her on social media.

Mumbai had long been considered a safe city, even the more deserted parts. It shook Vandana too, and she told me about an experiment she had conducted in Pune.[7] On 27 August 2013, at around 1 p.m., she took a ten-minute walk in a fairly well-to-do neighbourhood. She simply counted how many women and men she saw out on the streets during that walk, and the kinds of looks she got on the walk. The results were shocking: 147 men and 22 women. Of the women 18 were alone and rushing somewhere. Only four women were in a group together, chatting, whereas there were clumps of men hanging around chaiwallahs or just with their bikes. She noticed their continual glances at her and other women, which was deeply off-putting. It was not that anything happened, but it was just the feeling of being in a glass bowl and being stared at. This is the culture that we have. If it is unsafe for our girls to go out, why don't we keep the men at home?

The experiment provides an interesting insight: men generally take up more public space than women do. In the office, on the streets, on the metro (look at the queues for men compared to women), in restaurants and bars—pretty much everywhere. And over time, they have come to believe that it is their right to occupy that space.

So, this whole thing about being dressed in a certain way or not going out at night actually is not a problem about the dress or the time, but about women being in public spaces and taking up space. Men are simply not used to it. To be honest, women aren't used to it either. We are living through a great transition. That is why it is hyper important, in this transition period itself, that we lay down certain ground rules. We have to alter these age-old perceptions to establish a new norm.

At a time where the safety of women is an all-time high priority, it is also the perfect time to question how to resolve this issue. It must change if we want to live in an equitable world where everyone is respected. Women should be visible, listened to and included. It is only then that they will be respected everywhere and become an integral part of the community.

Currently, however, it is unsafe for women to be out in the streets, and there are very few of them being heard. We encourage our girls to spend as little time as possible outside. So, what self-fulfilling prophecy are we creating?

I wanted to do something about this. So, I thought to myself, 'Why haven't these molesters been caught? Why don't women call them out?'

I went around asking several women. It was a touchy subject, but some spoke up loudly. They said, 'Don't be ridiculous. How can we possibly call "them" out? We get pinched on our backside or elbowed in our breast, but *it is always in a crowd*. How do we catch the man if we don't know who he is?'

Always one to be a provoker, I thought of a simple sting operation. I went to the home minister of Maharashtra and said, 'This is my idea to catch "sexual harassers". I need to have police officers in plain clothing. That's all I need. They will walk behind our decoy girl, who is dressed reasonably, nothing too sexy. She goes into a crowd where we know there's been complaints of harassment. The two cops will be walking behind her and one of my volunteers will be walking around with a camera. As soon as she gets pinched, she'll cry out, and the two policemen will grab him. The volunteer will take a photo of the person as soon as he is nabbed by the police. A case will then be filed against him under Section 354 of the Indian Penal Code[8] and the police will take him to the police station. The offence is sometimes non-bailable, and as a punishment, he can be imprisoned for one to five years.'

But more importantly, the photo of the harasser is crucial. I said that we wanted to get the media involved. Only if the case was recorded by the police would the media publish his photo with genuine accusations of 'sexual harassment'. When this comes out, his mother will be horrified and say, 'What the hell were you doing?' God forbid if he is married, because his wife will be livid and consider leaving him. Neighbours will say, 'I'm never coming to this house again and my daughter will never see this boy.' He gets socially ostracized as well as faces a potential prison sentence. Once it's published that this can happen to you, sexual harassment in public spaces will decrease drastically, because it will no longer be considered 'worth it'. To make this a reality, there would have to be a consistent campaign by the government where they unequivocally say that they will no longer tolerate harassment in public places.

The home minister liked the idea but unfortunately, it was never fully carried out—budgets and some such rubbish stopped it. *However, with the growing voice of women's rights, perhaps it is time to reconsider. If we are really serious about getting rid of this menacing attitude, can we make this happen now?*

The Shame of WoMEN, Rape and #metoo

I was at a workshop on Shakespeare's poem, *The Rape of Lucrece*. At the end of it, we had a discussion, and I brought up the point that in those days and until today, women were ashamed that they had been raped. The biggest impact on them was the guilt they felt. The second impact was that they felt inferior to other women; they became more vulnerable than they already were. They felt as if they had become lesser human beings. The blame and shame of rape was somehow on them and, as a result, women were pushed into a slavish position, with this Sword of Damocles hanging over their heads. Rape is a strong power symbol.

Throughout our patriarchal history, women have been kept in their place by rape—don't do anything too bold because you could become an easy target; don't wear anything too revealing or go out too late, because you will send the signal you are loose, therefore anybody's prey. And aren't those bloody terrorists continuing the same thinking today? They rape the women in cities that they conquer, not necessarily because they enjoy sex, but because they want to ultimately subdue the will of the women.

It is not just terrorists. Remember the archaic practice of Sati, in Hindu culture, where a woman was supposed to sacrifice herself on the funeral pyre, should her husband die before her? What, so the life of a woman was worthless without a man? There is so much superstition in this country, but we call it 'tradition'. From what I understand, Indian organizations did not call for the ban (although Ram Mohan Roy was certainly very vocal about it)— historical records show it was Christian evangelists like William Carey who helped stamp out this awful practice by bringing in a law in 1829.[9] It was only in 1987 that it was officially criminalized in India. Yet another example of women being second-class citizens.

What about the men who control the casting couch in Bollywood and Hollywood? Aren't they also keeping women in their place? What about them using sex as a way to decide who gets what part in a movie? The countless starry-eyed girls who land up in Bombay not realizing what it is really all about. They end up falling in love with Bollywood knowing that Bollywood is full of pimps. They know it at the back of their mind, but they are so hungry for fame they are often willing to be pimped in the process. It is all about using women.

And this was ALL true, until recently.

One tiny but incredibly important change has come in.

Today, the anger that has always been there has come out into the open—it's more *visible*. While the feminist movement has been around for many years, this time the press and media are continually following it and women are being encouraged to openly express their anger in a way they never had the opportunity to do before.

In the past, women accepted that there was something called rape and they were sometimes subjected to it. Many powerful men were protected by their contacts. But today's (mainly privileged) women want to do something more radical about it by speaking up to those who will listen. They are turning on men and now saying, 'OK, if you think you can just assault her and nothing will happen, we'll show you that something *will* happen. We will put you in prison. You will lose elections.' (Well, maybe not). Look at Harvey Weinstein—he has lost his whole empire. He was one of the most powerful men in Hollywood, and now he is nothing. All because one woman found her voice and spoke out. Suddenly there's an avalanche and then it spreads like wildfire when others join in. Naming that person takes courage. Remember Madonna spoke out decades ago and said she was raped. But she did not name the person. A lot of people say they have been raped but stay quiet about who it was. The #metoo movement is all about naming a person, and that takes courage.

For the first time in modern history, the men are now publicly being shamed. The shame has moved from the woman being shamed for her body and for being a woman, to the men being exposed and shamed in their profession, with their profession itself being in danger. It is good to see that the media has taken up the calls of women and is giving them a chance to speak. Name and shame must continue. But it needs to extend to ALL strata of society, not just certain industries. The way rape cases like Shakti Mills were covered by the media led to a witch-hunt for rapists who are economically disadvantaged. But this masks the extent of violence that is much more prevalent and disturbing with those in power—think upper-class, higher-caste men or those with official positions, in the same way we talk about privileged white men.

For too long, the unchecked extent of violence in these groups has not been exposed. And it is time that it is and the less privileged women are given an equal voice.

Incidentally, we've always talked about women being raped. *Why are we not talking about men with misplaced power dominance? And what are we doing with the fact that men refuse to control themselves?*

Vandana tells me of of an Australian Journalist, Jane Gilmore, who is so infuriated with how the headlines reek of patriarchy that she has taken to re-titling the headlines and sending it back to the paper through her twitter handle @janegilmore. Here's an example:

NSW accountant jailed ~~over paid teen sex~~ **for sexual abuse and exploitation of teen girls**

Jane Gilmore's right, you know. This man did not 'have sex' with these teenagers, as if he was having a cup of tea. The man in question was fifty-eight years old. They were under seventeen, for God's sake. He groomed and raped them. It's like the phrase 'child prostitute'—come on, this is clearly an example of an older man in a position of power, exploiting someone much younger. It is the man at fault, yet the headline somehow makes it out to be something else.

So, we are turning the problem back to being about the perpetrators: the men. Turn the problem on its head and looking at it in a different way, because let's face it, men are the problem, women are not. Bizarrely, many people think that *Pirates of the*

Caribbean's Captain Jack Sparrow said the famous words, 'The problem is not the problem. The problem is your attitude to the problem.' He did not. It was in fact, a woman, Ann Brashares.[10] Kind of sums it up, doesn't it?

I am sure the women out there are agreeing with me while their male counterparts are looking at me, wide-eyed with horror. All their 'innocent' innuendos and accidental hand-scraping against women are harmless. Is it? How would you like it if the tables were turned?

But women, why are you not standing up *more* to stop this?

Women Hate Themselves: A World of False Promises

From women's eyes this doctrine I derive:
They sparkle still the right Promethean fire;
They are the books, the arts, the academes,
That show, contain, and nourish all the world.
                              —*Love's Labour's Lost*, Act IV, Scene III

Women are beginning to shoot to the front, but probably only over the last seventy-five years. For much of the past, the majority of women spent their time at home and being part of men's gossip. There were very few women who were published and credited for writing thought-leader-style books or given the opportunity to be educated to the same level as men. Vandana reminds me of Savitri Bai Phule, who is purported to be the 'first' female teacher of India. When did she live? In the mid-1850s. That was hardly 170 years ago. There would definitely have been other female teachers, but none that were considered significant. Same with female writers— so few were published a hundred years ago. And even if they were, they were always thought (by men) to be too light. The public impression was that the men wrote deep books and women wrote shallow books, which is not true at all!

It is great that women are now coming out of their private think-holes. Now we are beginning to see that women are equal to men, and in my opinion, in many ways superior. Go back to Simone de Beauvoir and Jean Paul Sartre—ah, there was an equal battle!

Overall, the problem is that women are generally second-guessing themselves in the workplace and whenever they are challenged by men. Because of their existing power in a patriarchal setup, men don't even question their own capabilities a lot of the time. Whereas women do and over-analyse. WHY? Vandana tells me there is research that is starting to show how much past trauma impacts future generations. So, generations of women being held back is automatically transferred into the subconscious thinking of the current generation. That may be the case, but women, how long are you going to allow yourselves to be subdued because of misdemeanours in the past?

The women in the *bastis* lament their husbands who have drunk themselves to near death, but they refuse to acknowledge that the women themselves have done a fabulous job of bringing up the family and keeping everyone together. They are so focused on how useless their husband is that they quite forget who the real heroes of the story are. And this pattern of women wanting men to take the lead and be responsible is repeated generation after generation, despite the women successfully taking the lead themselves and being responsible. In the workplace, women are often looking for validation for what they have done, often from men. Not realizing that those men, in my opinion, are insecure about them and their skills.

This transition period is the time that women must stand up to the false promises and lip service of a so-called equal and equitable world. Whatever the world is, it's 50 per cent yours. To hell with the men being on your side. Decondition your thinking, women! You don't need their support. Let's get rid of the myth that men are more important and that only men can do it and women cannot. Women, do not give men the licence to dominate. Not anymore.

Remember it is the mother who has the greatest influence on her children, whether male or female. The father does not. So, if a mother treats her son equally, then she can recondition both sexes to believe that men are not gods who will look after them no matter what. They are just one of the genders and have learnt skilfully to dominate this planet. Isn't it time to change that?

Extracting the Essence

» Gender is a social construct that men have used to their advantage for millennia.

» Today, men are dominating women psychologically more than physically, due to their own fears.

» Men are also victims of patriarchy.

» Men need to be recalibrated for today's woman.

» Women need to continue to stand up to and call out unacceptable behaviour.

» The media needs to take responsibility for the way it continues to portray women and for constantly perpetuating misogyny.

» Both men and women need to take a stand for equity and equality.

Hijacking Your Mind—Points for You to Ponder

» If you identify with being female, where are you playing the victim?

» If you identify with being male, where do you not stand up and support women?

» Why don't you write to the media when there is subliminal sexism?

» What unresolved gender constructs are holding you back? And what change can you make to overcome it?

5

Make Way for the
C?O instead of the CEO

AKA How Should Corporate Leaders Focus on Building
Sustainable Value for All Major Stakeholders?

The Amuse-Bouche of the Chapter: I Want a Better
Fruit for the World

Advertising has been in my blood for as long as I can remember.
And one of the reasons I was so successful at it was my ability
to take an idea or concept from one area and use it in a totally
different area. Take the common technique in marketing that gets
someone to imagine an object as something entirely different, to
get an idea of its relative position or a comparison for how good
or bad it is. For example, 'If a BMW was a fruit, then what fruit
would it be?' It would not be a lowly orange, that's for sure. It
would be something like a Densuke watermelon—dark and strong
on the outside, but mouth-watering and luxurious on the inside.

I like to use that technique for non-marketing purposes, to
help me understand the state of the world. For example, let's use
a similar analogy to the fruit to understand what our corporate

world is like. If the corporate world was a human being, then what kind of human being would it be? One way of considering this would be to go back to the earliest corporations and think about what they would be. So, if the birth of the corporate world dates back to the East India Company, we can imagine that at the beginning it would have been a wide-eyed, blue-eyed baby, full of all the wonder of the world before it. By the end of its years, the East India Company would have been an arrogant toddler who threw his toys out of the cot and then retreated into its cot in a huff (with all its toys and more).

By the same analogy, our corporate world today looks like an unruly, dissatisfied, rebellious teenager who has become a condescending young adult, foisting its views on everyone. And of course, the loudest voice becomes one of Voltaire's bastards, feeding the masses its dominant views of what success is and what people should be aiming for.

Cultures Grow

Sitting here in Mumbai, I feel that it is actually corporate culture that has the largest influence on the culture of humanity today. As human beings, we tend to subconsciously reflect the prevailing corporate culture. Whether we talk about the race for who has the largest bank account and most assets or the greatest success (proved by the largest car or house), we tend to emulate what we are seeing around us in corporate culture. And because American companies are global as well as 'loud' (compared to their Chinese counterparts), the culture of humanity today is pretty much being dictated by American company culture and the American people. I don't necessarily mean it in a bad sense, but let's face it, American culture is driven by the 'constantly improve and constantly grow' formula. Often, they don't mean 'grow' in the best sense of the word.

They mean commercial growth.

And because of this, GNP or gross national product dominates everything today in the world. A primary symbol in the modern world of this growth?

NYSE.

If you really think about it, the Big Board of the New York Stock Exchange has actually formed the culture of the world. Every country is constantly trying to do better, get richer and do more to catch up with America. That's also what the people of the world are trying to do. Automatically, without thinking, like hamsters on a wheel!

I want to ask you, in what sense should we be 'doing better'? In the sense of money and power? Those are the two overriding principles of today's world. If that's the case, it's a pretty bad culture because nobody is ever satisfied.

I think I have finally realized the real villain is this promulgated idea that *everything must be better*. It's epitomized by the ubiquitous cell phone. Hardly have they brought out one iPhone, information about the next is already being leaked! And because people have to be the best—better than anyone else—they have to upgrade. This creates a vicious circle of wanting to have the 'best' at all times and running after anything to get it.

But for God's sake, can people start shouting about what's wrong with that approach? I mean, it's nice to do 'better' because we progress. See how far the lowly cell phone has come. From just receiving a call, you can now order food, pay your grocery bill, check your bank balance—you can do almost everything with it.

But wait.

Do you notice how they are always adding some other feature to it that we did not know we wanted? We are always waiting for the next marvellous thing and the marvellous thing is always to do with some kind of gain outside of yourself. Somebody else is making money out of you or using your personal details to collect more information about you. They don't really care about what *you* want, as long as they can make money out of you. The gods that we worship today are money and power. These are false gods because they don't bring you happiness. As soon as you get money you want more money . . .

ALYQUEISM: To execute is to KILL. It's time to stop killing the workplace with rules that make people unhappy and start creating a place that all stakeholders want to flock to.

Money Money Money

Money: that elusive substance that rules our lives. I got quite an insight into money when I was invited to a boring sit-down dinner at the Calcutta Club many years ago. The guy next to me, who shall remain unnamed, was a billionaire. I said, 'XX Ji, you have a lot of money. What do you do with this money?'

He looked at me astonished and said, 'Padamsee sir, what do I do with my money? I make more money.'

I replied, 'Yes, but what do you do with your "more" money?'

He stared me straight in the eye and said, 'Make more money.'

I persisted, 'In the end, don't you want to *do* something with that money?'

He looked confused and said, 'Ha. Perhaps.'

But you see, making *more* money was the name of the game.

What I'm saying is we're all in the rat race and we all want money or power. Power is often shown through a promotion at work, as that leads to more money as well. We're not saying, 'I've got a lovely job. I'm enjoying it. And if they offer me a promotion, I know I would refuse it.' We are driven by money and senior positions of power. As I said before, we get caught up in the hamster wheel, where we are trying to go faster than everyone around us in the hope that we will 'do better'.

Here's the harsh truth. The net result is that nobody is happy. Not the richest person in the world or the poorest, or anyone in between. Believe me, I've spent time with royalty and rural roamers. They are all caught up in this idea of 'doing better' and keep fighting forward. Vandana says it's like everyone is on the circular motorway outside of London, the M25, going really fast and trying to overtake each other, not realizing they are going round and round and no one is getting off.

Which is why I believe that what you should be thinking about is, '*What is happiness for me?*' Because isn't that what life is really about?

Just stop for a minute and think about what modern life is like today. You get up in the morning. You brush your teeth, have a shower, get dressed, have breakfast. You then rush to the office. You sit at your desk and get onto that computer. Before you know it, you've been in three meetings, dealt with emails but done hardly any real work before lunch. You then gobble down your lunch, answer more emails and have more meetings. Then you look at the clock, and it's past home time. You drive home. You say hi to the spouse and kids. You have dinner. Watch a couple of shows on the TV. Yawn. You go to bed. You then get up the following morning. You brush your teeth, have a shower . . .

Goodness, is this happiness? Is this what we want for ourselves AND for the next generation of humanity? Really?

The Starter Course: Happiness Is in Feeling at Home

Don't you think it's time for a new definition of culture? What about a culture of spreading happiness? Actually, I think it is more about how to 'ignite happiness', to run a collision course to create happiness. I mean, whatever you do and wherever you go, ignite happiness. As I said earlier, the prevailing culture comes from corporate culture. So if we make changes in the workplace in our goals and the way we treat people, we will also be able to influence the rest of humanity, wherever they are in the world.

This goes back to a talk I gave in Pune at the British Business Group. It was called 'Strangers in the Home' because that's what's happened—we have become complete strangers in the home. And part of that is because we are also strangers in the office. We have brought that culture home with us and have forgotten what it's like to be part of the family.

My philosophy has always been that a company is really a collection of people who have a common purpose and who are not there primarily to make profits, though most of you may disagree. I believe it is to bring together people with the aims and objectives of enjoying their work, so that it in turn pays rich dividends, both in the workplace and at home.

I honestly believe leaders themselves should be curious and not suspicious, thinking 'how will my people benefit?'. I talked at length in my last book *A Double Life* about my work at Lintas. At Lintas, I didn't like the idea of an office being an office. I wanted an office to be a home where people felt nurtured and stimulated to think differently. I was ready to let them change the environment. I had a policy of allowing them to choose their own furniture for their cabins, and I gave each executive a budget every year to decorate his cabin any way they liked. It went beyond paintings. Someone even had roller skates at work—anything they liked that made them feel exhilarated to be there!

It had not always been that way. To use the previous analogy of a company as a human being, when I arrived at Lintas, it was already a fuddy-duddy old man dressed in a five-piece suit and a bowler hat, with his nose turned up and an eyepiece to magnify everything anyone did with a dreadful shake of the head. It was completely outdated for what we were doing. It was very much on the lines of Hindustan Lever, which once owned Lintas and had a lot of rules and regulations. I'll give you an example. If you wanted to get a pencil, you had to sign three forms and get three signatures. Even though it was the 1980s, Lintas was very much driven by the red tape of the 1940s.

When I got the top job (see the 'dessert section' at the end of this chapter), I was determined to remind the old man Lintas that he could shake off his garb and be a hip and happening teenager Lintas. And remember, teenagers are all about friendships. So I said, 'I'm going to try and remake the entire business model.' The first thing I said we're going to do is become *friends*. I find that the larger the company, the more the rivalry. Colleagues are not help-mates, but hell-mates. Everyone wants to get ahead of the next guy/girl sitting next to him/her, in the next place or the next cabin. And that leads to a lot of animosity.

I wanted my employees to feel like my family, not competitive robots.

So I asked my people, 'How many of you suffer from Monday morning blues?' There was a big laugh, with lots of agreement.

I said, 'We're going to change that to "red carpet Monday mornings". How are we going to do that? By getting all of you together on the landing of the lift on Monday morning. And sharp at 9.30 no one goes to their cabin for the first half an hour. Tea and snacks will be served, and we'll just relax. We spend more time in this place than we do at home, so it should have a nice family atmosphere. From next Monday morning, I suggest we talk about what we did on the weekend. Did you do anything interesting? Some people enjoy hobbies, and I'm a big hobbies fan. I think that hobbies lessen the tensions of work. You should be able to side-step from work and do what gives you pleasure—and that's hobbies. From next Monday, you are going to tell us what your hobby is and what you did over the weekend . . .'

This actually got people talking to each other. Normally, they'd just go to their desk, pick up their phone and start ordering people around. This informal meet gave them a chance to talk to their colleagues. We started with department heads and after about two to three weeks, everybody really began to enjoy it. And they got to know the person in the next cabin whom they hadn't actually spoken to for at least two months. And now they're on first-name terms, sharing things like 'my hobby and your hobby'. And this led to a very friendly atmosphere. People now began to treat other people not as rivals, but as people who they had shared something important with. Sharing is a very natural human tendency if we allow it. Unfortunately, in today's Americanized world, it is difficult because everyone wants to get ahead. They may get ahead and have a heart attack in the process, but they still won't stop. I thought that's a very wrong way to go about one of the most important things in your life after your family, which is your work.

The result was a superb increase in profits and an abundance of awards. If you concentrate on happiness, magic happens.

The Soup Course: What Is the C?O?

As Lintas proved back in the 1980s and 1900s, the world does not HAVE to be about everything being 'better' and people don't HAVE to run directly after money and power. We can say NO. The people who need to do that are the people running those corporations that are the equivalent of surly, rebellious teenagers today. It is time to come out of your surliness and become the adult we all need in our life—one that understands what his or her employees want deep inside. That starts with the CEO saying NO to that American culture of 'do better' and turning it into the employee culture of 'being happier'.

I can tell you from my own experience both in advertising and on the stage that when people are happy, their work becomes their worship. Literally . . . but you've got to *stimulate* them to enjoy their work and then it becomes worship. Which is why I say CEO, make way for the CSO the Chief Stimulation Officer!

When I saw myself as the Chief Stimulation Officer is when I actually fell in love with Lintas. It became more important in my life than my wife Dolly, who I was with at that time. It became more important than my children, it became my most loved child. Every day I got up thinking, how can I make things more motivational? How can I be the Chief Stimulation Officer that people will actually be stimulated by?

Other stimulations:

» We abolished the term 'Sir'.
» My cabin was like my family drawing room, complete with a rocking chair and a rowing machine.
» We rented a holiday home for all employees, from MD to peon.
» We started a hobby club.
» We cleared space for a Zen room.
» We started lunch time stimulation sessions.
» We started a Lintas Cricket Team and rented practice nets.
» We started a Lintas Year-End Party.
» We didn't have a sexual counselling manager, but we should have had one.

In my terminology, we were not fixated on GNP but on creating gross national happiness within the office. In five years, Lintas moved from No.5 to No.1 and tripled its turnover. With fewer, better motivated people, we made ten times the profit of the other leading agencies. Our attrition rate came down to 15 per cent, as opposed to the industry rate of 35 per cent. And we had a number of boomerangs too: people who left and came back, as they missed the happiness culture too much.

When I was preparing for the session at the British Business Group in Pune, it also ignited in my mind what the outcome of that happiness is. If people are happy (and are kept happy), they are more productive. Productive can mean love, productive can mean money, productive can mean anything. I did this both in Lintas and in the theatre: kept people happy. I was the chief stimulator in both.

Writing this, I realize that all my life I have been chasing happiness. I had three marriages and I had several long-term involvements, and I've always found that I was interested in ensuring the other person was happy. When people are happy, I think they feel they are growing.

So, I think the future will be no longer the CEO's but the CSO's—Chief Stimulation Officers who are all the time throwing ideas at their team and opening windows so that they can open doors.

The Main Course: The Question in C?O

As I have been writing this book with Vandana, it has become apparent to me that it is not just about stimulation. The CEO needs to give up this idea of executing—as we all know from history, execution and executioners are all about death. And we don't want companies to die but thrive. So we have come up with some other words that the '?' could be replaced with. Try these for size, swim about in them and see what wonders they bring to your employees. Then watch how the rest of the world adopts good techniques to create a happier world.

CVO
You know, there was something magical about the plays I was involved in. We may have had the same number of actors and production staff, but we managed to do some of the longest runs

in the history of Indian theatre. Just like many of the commercials that our team made lasted for decades.

It's because everything I did was about VALUE. I ensured that people were really involved in the work we were doing—they saw the value for themselves as well as others. By having three months of sessions with the actors and actresses, before even starting rehearsals, they got to know the play and characters so well that production became easier. I was the Chief Value Officer.

CCO (Chief Creative Officer)

My experience has shown me that everyone has another side to them. From our peons to our senior directors at Lintas, people were happiest when they felt fulfilled. Those who were not getting it from work would be encouraged to find it outside of work and, as I mentioned, share it at work as part of Red-Carpet Mondays. So, helping others be CREATIVE and discover their interests is part of what a C?O should do. People blossom when they are creative. It is your job to shower them with appreciation for it and then sit back and watch them bloom. I was the Chief Creative officer.

CRO

Failure is such a tough word in the workplace. You know we're always taught not to fail, but actually CEOs need to fail because that's how they REINVENT and REIMAGINE. One of my heroes, Edison, said words to the effect of, 'I have not failed. I've just found 10,000 ways that won't work.' So the job of the C?O is to reinvent when things have not worked out the way we want. Confidence is about not being worried about failure. Because there is always another way out. I was that Chief Reinvention Officer.

CASO

I was invited to be on the advisory board of IIT Bombay, an institution revered all over the world as well as in India. Someone asked the head of IIT why I was offered the position. According to this gentleman, I was a particularly good creative man, but the rest of the board were all engineers and/or alumni. The head of IIT said that it was because I was good at coming up with ALTERNATIVE SOLUTIONS. At the time, the people at IIT were worried about cash, as they were reliant only on government funding, which was being cut, and they were looking for alternatives. So, I said, 'Well you have your own funding. You have fantastic collateral.'

The head said, 'Collateral? What collateral? We don't have any.'

I said, 'Your alumni! Your alumni are heading some of the biggest companies in America, in England, in Germany and all over the world and they will be incredibly happy to contribute towards their alma mater. It's their mother, it's what made them who they are today.'

I had done my homework. I had asked a few of them and they had said, 'My goodness, we haven't been asked to donate, but if we are asked, we definitely would.'

Within a few years, suddenly so many buildings sprang up. Laboratories, auditoriums, all sorts of things. And even tennis courts and leisure activities so that the students felt people cared for them. Another advantage was that the IITs were able to do the kind of research and development that big companies wanted. All from the alternative thinking perspective. I was most certainly the Chief Alternative Solutions Officer.

CViO

It is not enough for a C?O to be just running the company. They have to be able to future-proof the life of that company. They have to be able to predict how the company will stay afloat even in unexpected times. They need to be a VISIONARY. In both my plays and in advertising, I had to be able create the vision before others could see it. If I had the vision and could explain it to them in glorious detail, the team would be able to deliver it. And that they did, day after day, year after year and decade after decade. I was the Chief Visionary Officer.

CDO

It is not enough to be creative and visionary though when you are in a senior position. Sometimes thoughts get left out as 'pie in the sky' if they are not developed properly. The C?O must be DISCIPLINED, even when it comes to creativity. Creative freedom by itself is great, but you need discipline. And when you say 'I'm not willing to define that', it's not discipline. I was involved in every part of our campaigns. As a CDO you've got to take the bull by the horns, write it down and go through the whole process in minute detail. Do not leave anything to chance. You have to be willing to get not just your hands dirty, but every part of your body needs to be sunk in the muck, if you are going to produce something that is worth remembering.

When it came to theatre, I would consistently tell everyone, 'Rehearse, rehearse, rehearse and keep rehearsing until you get it right, and after you get it right, rehearse once more.' And that is why our productions ran on and on. Because believe you me, I was the Chief Disciplinarian (let's dispense with officer here!).

CIO

As a CEO, let me remind you again, you execute nothing! Your job is to IMPROVE the conditions under which workers work, IMPROVE the product or service itself. You are the Chief Improvement Officer. You are the future-proofer. If you get it wrong, the whole company collapses, and with that the lives of your employees. So improve, improve, improve. And IMAGINE too—that is one of the biggest gifts that humanity has: the ability to improve and imagine.

Living the C?O in Practice

Ashwini Deshpande
Co-founder, Multiple Award-Winning Elephant Design

As impressionable students at National Institute of Design in the eighties, we did not want to join advertising. Design was 'user-focused' and advertising was considered too 'commercial'. But progressive leaders like Alyque realized the value designers could add to the field. So he had sent a senior team member from Lintas to speak to us in Ahmedabad and convince us to check it out. I took the bait and was welcomed as an intern at Lintas Mumbai in 1986.

Express Towers was a buzzing place and there was no dearth of exciting work at Lintas. But what I remember the most was its culture. The launch of an ad or winning an account was celebrated with gusto. Alyque would frequently walk through the maze of cubicles and enquire what's up. If he saw a huddle, he would join in and share an idea or two. If he heard some agitated accounts executive on a phone call, he would pat their back and move on. However, the most amazing time was Friday evenings. I distinctly remember Alyque standing at the corner of the studio, clapping and saying, 'It's the weekend, guys.' And then there would be an impromptu gathering in the big hall. Beer and wafers would appear in no time. The party would go on till someone would head back to finish work.

It made me realize that Lintas did not need formal team-building initiatives. It was achieved through big and small everyday acts of spontaneity and empathy. And that was Alyque's touch.

Dessert: Stimulating Down the Toilet

Stimulation of business was critical when I took over. We were trying to shed our old image and be seen as innovative. That year, we had Rs. 5,00,000 as the total bonus for the office to share.

Everyone said, 'Well, let's give a big party to the clients.'

I thought that was boring, and my mind started to wander. I was wondering what we all shared that we could improve on. And then I hit upon that crazy idea. It's only because I was at the Oberoi Hotel that afternoon, where they have fantastic bathrooms—the best in Mumbai. I said, 'Let's spend the whole lot on the loo. Everyone has to go to the loo at some point. So why not spend it on the loo?'

Everyone thought I had gone mad, but I pushed through with it. We did up the loo and it looked incredible! We even had a pooja when we opened it, and everyone was there to watch.

I realized that we had to have our loo talked about. So I engineered a meeting with the chairman of Unilever. In those days, we would invite him to the office once a year and do a showreel of all their adverts. It was an exceptionally long meeting, and I kept on plying him with coffee and water. After about two hours, he said, 'Excuse me, I have to go to the loo.' I said casually, 'Go out, turn right, then you come to the loo.'

Well, we all waited anxiously for him to come back. He came back into the room looking gobsmacked.

He said, 'My God.'

I said, 'What is it?'

He said, 'What a fantastic loo you have.'

Everyone was trying to hide their laughter as they knew I had set this up.

He said, 'You must be doing very well to have a loo like that.' Luckily, he hadn't seen the rest of the office—it was pretty drab. We didn't have the money at that time to do up the whole office. But this toilet was the showpiece.

He said, 'Lintas is doing very well, congratulations.'

And then he went around telling other people—his business acquaintances, the Rotary Club and so on—that Lintas was doing extremely well, they should do advertising with us, we really knew how to do it.

Then we had lots of people coming in just to look at the loo! And business boomed.

Ah. Stimulation.

Flashback!

How did I become the head of Lintas? Let's hear directly from Gerson Da Cunha, the great theatre personality and advertising guru.

'I was back in India after two years, during which I was on leave in Brazil from the agency. Alyque was running the place in my absence as deputy manager (DM). I told him I wanted to visit the agency. Without my knowledge, he gathered everybody in the reception area to welcome me. But I had a full bladder when I got to the thirteenth floor and, without looking to the right or left, I raced to the loo. They waited patiently and applauded when I showed up. Briefly, then, I told them about my spell in Brazil, about my doing an assignment for UNICEF which ended up with them offering me a job in the UN. I was excited by the challenge and confident that I was leaving my old job in the most competent of hands, Alyque's. There were great cheers from the gathering. After I was through, Dr Ranjan Banerjee, Chairman of Lintas and Personnel Director of Hindustan Lever, drew me aside. 'Has Lintas London approved your succession and Alyque's appointment?' he asked. They had not, because I had not consulted them. Alyque was a leading figure in Indian advertising, had spent 20 years in Lintas and was very interested in the job. (He had earlier asked to be named my DM.) That evening, at tea for everybody on the top floor of Express Towers, with a few clients present, I repeated the essence of my morning's talk, to be then embraced a bit emotionally by Alyque.'

Over a period of fourteen years, Lintas became a brand. And in the process, I became known as Mr Advertising because we were making a tidy profit. I explained this when I spoke at the British Business Group in Pune. It became a watershed moment for many of those who came: I said GNH (gross national happiness) results in GNP (gross national profit). The members had never looked at it that way before.

Lintas became a legacy of being an enriching environment. I love that word 'enrich'. And I found that people from Lintas were almost like people in college, thinking of us as their alma mater. Even now when I meet them, like thirty years later, they say, 'Alyque, those days were wonderful and we never wanted to leave Lintas, because it was like our home.'

Live Lightly

Gurcharan Das
Former CEO, Proctor & Gamble

What a daring and exciting thought of Alyque's: A company is a collection of people who come together for enjoying themselves, then becoming friends and finally making money as a by-product. Alyque is spot-on in wanting to get rid of the old command and control culture. The ultimate secret I believe lies in learning to live lightly, not like a feather but as a bird. This is only possible if one takes ones' work seriously but not oneself seriously.

After-Dinner Coffee: Creating the Ripple

You know, igniting happiness is never just about the people around you. It is for society as well. Once I got this job and I was earning money, I had the feeling that all this money was not just for me or for my family. That's when I began getting involved with anything to do with public service. And I took it upon myself to do just that, in the best way I could. I opened a division of Lintas for public service provision, and I got my board of directors to donate 2 per cent of the profit we made every year to this division. We could do activities pro bono for causes because the profit we were making was pretty hefty. You'll read about the public service division and activities in some of the other chapters.

The beauty of it was that everyone involved with the public service work poured their heart and soul into it, sometimes even more so, as if the NGOs were paying customers. And they went home happier for it, spreading joy all around.

A right judgement draws us a profit from all things we see.
—*Romeo and Juliet*, Act I, Scene I

Extracting the Essence

» The world is like a dissatisfied, rebellious, entitled teenager.
» Constantly growing is not a recipe for humanity's success.
» Happiness and belonging, both in the workplace and at home, make up success, not money.
» Rethinking titles will give us a better sense of how we can create happiness and belonging.
» The loo is more important than you give it credit for.
» Public service ignites happiness.

Hijacking Your Mind—Points for You to Ponder

» What culture are you growing in all your circles?
» Which one is your favourite C?O title and why?

» What should your title really be? And what actions will you
  take to make it happen?
» What does money buy you?

6

Change the Battlefield

Selling the Truth

Compress Those Compartments and Reformat Your Life!

We have an overload of information every minute of the day. Whether it is from our mobile phones, on television, from the meetings we have at the office, or Friday night drinks, we are always talking about areas that interest us. But most conversations tend to follow a very linear theme. We start off by talking about the weather, then move on to politics, then may be come to something we saw on television. It is all very straight-line thinking isn't it? One topic at a time, thank you very much and then on to the next.

I blame the newspapers for starting the trend of linear thinking and linear conversations.

'Don't be ridiculous Alyque!' I hear you say. 'You seem to be blaming the media for quite a lot. Surely you can't blame them for the way we think overall?'

Well yes, I can, and I'll explain my logic. I am specifically talking about newspapers for linear thinking, mind you, not the media in general.

Ponder for a second on how we got the news in the old days. First, there was pigeon mail. Then there was pony mail. Then the printing press was invented. The next stage of getting news was the advent of the newspaper. Through printing presses, hundreds of copies of newspapers could be sent out to everyone at the same time. But they had to find a way to share the news in a sensible way. The newspaper was formatted in a certain way, with a front page and important news headlines, the next page with less important news, then social news, then sports and it went on, dividing life into compartments.

It actually formatted your life, as you read it every day. So, you began to think like that. You would think, 'What's most important to me?' After pondering: 'The political situation, Yeah. Then the business situation, then the sports section.' Then we began to think like newspapers. In compartments and boxes. Next to those compartments were other compartments with advertising, which told us what to think about when we weren't thinking about the news in the newspapers. It might have been, 'Get a great body by drinking this tonic' or 'Wear this watch and get the spouse of your dreams', and other such illusions. So we got reformatted to consider the newspaper compartments first, then the advertising compartments second. The format of our thinking before that was that there was no format of thinking.

Am I right or wrong?

This book talks about how to reformat your brain from being in confined compartments and thinking in straight lines to thinking in squiggly lines. However, this chapter is special to me. It's where I show you how you can use the principles of advertising to help you get whatever you want in life. I want you to see that you can change the battlefield and learn from the masters on how to do so.

'The medium is not the message, but the medium is the MASSAGE.'

The Elixir of Life: Words and Symbols

Make no mistake, whenever you want to get anything done with the help of others, you have to use the principles of advertising. Think about it. If you are a wife and want to go out with the girls for the night, what do you do? You say to your husband, 'Honey, wouldn't you like a night in, just for yourself? No one to hassle you. Wouldn't that be nice?' Or you might say, 'Darling, isn't it time you went out with the boys? You haven't seen them for a while, and wouldn't it be nice to sink a few beers with them? Why don't you do that tonight?' And lo and behold, you have altered your husband's thoughts on a night alone without you, freeing you up to do what you want. You have just used the tenets of advertising.

You see words and symbols are to humans what sunlight is to a flower: the reason for growth. And there's no place better than advertising to show you how to be inspired and grow.

What Is Advertising?

And oftentimes, to win us to our harm,
The instruments of darkness tell us truths,
Win us with honest trifles, to betray's
In deepest consequence.

—*Macbeth*, Act I, Scene III

Encyclopaedia Britannica says advertising is 'The techniques and practices used to bring products, services, opinions, or causes to public notice for the purpose of persuading the public to respond in a certain way toward what is advertised.'[1]

I say, rubbish.

Advertising is simply how you make a product or service more attractive than it currently is, thereby motivating and inspiring someone to use it.

Like telling your husband that a few hours without you could be a good thing, and that he could do so much with it which would benefit *him*, thereby motivating him. If that isn't using advertising philosophy, what is?

Let's get back to the kind of advertising I did for much of my life, because it relates to why I wrote this book. I think I was so successful at it because I could persuade others to think completely differently about a subject. I would hijack the consumer's mind. I did it in a way that was remarkably original and not clichéd. I hope the examples in this chapter will give you an insight into my style of advertising and, in doing so, will help you create ways of changing the battlefield in your most important asset: *your head*. As Vandana often tells me, people are good at cleansing their bodies but polluting their minds.

Perhaps you can use this chapter as a way to bring inspiration and growth to yourself and all around you.

Clichés Kill

And here is the first rule of advertising. Most people ignore it, but the rule is, 'Kill the cliché before it kills you.' For example, think of the first thought that comes to mind with the advent of the mobile phone. The first thought was, 'I can get America with just the touch of a button.' So many in the industry said that the catchphrase should be, 'Get America with the touch of one button.'

I said that's a cliché. It doesn't motivate people. It only informs them about what they can do. Advertising is *not there to inform alone: it should be inspiring enough to motivate them to try it*. I would say to that person, 'Go start again. You're going the easy route. People usually say the first thing that come into their mind. It is the most obvious, so the wrong thing to think. Kill that!'

So how about making the mobile phone not about you being able to get in touch with others, but others that you care about being able to get in touch with you? What about doing a campaign on giving a mobile phone to your old mom who will just be so grateful that she can be in touch with her adult children again? That is much more inspiring.

So when you are in a conversation and trying to win an argument, can you kill the clichés of the argument and find a way to inspire instead?

Emotional Currents

I approach advertising in different ways. I've already told you about one I use a lot: emotional logic. I like to think I have used it to stir up the right sentiments to motivate people. It is one of the most vicious and most sympathetic as well as empathetic theories I've used. If done subtly, I find emotional logic can change a whole nation. So it can definitely change the people around you if you apply it.

Here's an example of how emotional logic changed a nation. The Germans, after the First World War, were decimated by the allies, who really extracted their vengeance through the treaty of Versailles. Hitler came, and his main point was 'we are a united Germany', but he needed a good slogan. His slogan was 'Germany above all. We are the master race. We are the people who should rule the world.'

That man was one of the most powerful prophets for a beaten nation. A small army but a great force that was in the form of a man: a saviour for them, if you will. And for people who had been defeated in the war, who were starving and facing sky-high inflation, it was what they needed emotionally. The famous example was if you ordered a loaf of bread, you borrowed your neighbour's wheelbarrow, put all your oats in it, wheeled it to the shop to buy that loaf of bread. That was what was happening in Germany after the First World War. No one can believe that in Germany today!

Hitler took that opportunity of people being defeated and used pure emotional logic. They were not the master race in most people's opinion. They had just been defeated in a war, but that triggered the fact that, inherent in the German psyche, was the feeling that they make better products, better factories etc. and they did, but they had lost it all in the war. And now suddenly here was this man, a brilliant speaker, who just fired them up with emotional logic. Everything he said was 'we shall'. He never said, 'I shall.' He said, 'We will be the master race.' How he masterminded the Nazi idea! Long before advertising people discovered that it is very nice to have mugs with your product on it in different forms and other such giveaways, Hitler's team was doing it. Goebbels, his propaganda minister, did nothing but advertising. And made films. 'We are the master race,' the films said. And in the films, there was not a single black-haired person. They were all blonde: the women were blonde, the children were blonde, shopkeepers were blonde. He had this idea of the 'Aryan Race'. He himself had black hair, but he went against it.

Yeah. A masterstroke for emotional logic. Hitler was selling.

Advertising happens all the time in politics and creates false gods. I talked about worshipping false gods, and one of the false gods we must talk about is Donald Trump. In Donald Trump, America elected a man who is now being called insane . . . and is a fine example of worshipping false gods, where emotional logic wins over logic.

Look at what he's saying. I've been following Donald Trump from his first day until today. He's a very original thinker, but unconventional. People immediately dismiss him as a kind of fool. Take this thing about white supremacy. I can tell you, in America,

70–80 per cent of white people would never allow their white daughter to marry a black man. You can say what you like, but Donald Trump has revealed that a number of white Americans are actually supremacists, and they don't like the black man. They don't like them for any logical reason—it is purely in their cultural DNA. It's a really dangerous thing to say, but it's true. This has come to my mind because of Charlottesville. Trump has an uncanny knack of disrobing conventional ideas and selling an old story. And small-town white Americans are against anyone who does not look or talk like them: they are essentially racist. Trump panders to them with his emotional logic. He is the king of emotional logic of the small-town white American who feels forgotten. He is selling to them, because they are his vote bank.

Have you noticed that that this theme runs through all my ideas? I'm always asking what and why people are selling. And if you go through all my advertising ideas, I always hijack the view or change the battlefield, to get people to see things from a different angle. When I came up with the Kama Sutra example, up until then, everyone was selling condoms for safety, not for sex. And I said, 'Sell it for sex because the only time you wear a condom is when you're having sex.' I changed the whole battleground from safety to sex appeal with Kama Sutra condoms.[2]

So, how can you use emotional logic rather than rational logic to get decisions pushed through at work or get your family to agree to something? Doesn't it tug on the heartstrings much more and aren't the results more effective?

The Medium Is the Massage

My great guru, whom I've never mentioned, is a guy called Marshall McLuhan. He was a very original thinker. I discovered him in the 1980s. He was a media and communications expert, and he said things like, 'The medium is not the message, but the medium is the *massage*.'³ The medium massages you into believing things that you would normally not believe. He was talking about television media at that time and predicted the web thirty years before it existed.

But now, social media and Donald Trump have taught me that social media has become more important than mass media. It is an important point that politicians and anyone who wants to create change have to know: they must get into social media. Writing an article in the newspaper is great, but there's only a limited number of people who read it. Most of them, unfortunately and honestly, are getting older and dying off. But all young people are in the social media arena. My daughter says, 'Dad, why do you read a newspaper? I get the news before you. Right here on my phone.'

Without the media on your side, you are invisible. I learnt that in advertising: any venture that doesn't advertise will go bankrupt very fast. Advertising will get you a sale, telling people why a product is excellent and how it can do you good. And if you want, you can add an emotional benefit like I have done in many cases. Liril soap is for freshness and the bath you take with Liril soap gives you freshness, but Liril has a perfume that makes you *feel* fresh. So while you're having a bath, you start imagining the commercial which everyone used to see on the TV, which is the 'girl in the waterfall'. She was simply jumping around, dancing and laughing. There was no boyfriend. There was nothing—just her. So using the media, we're able to propagate new ideas. But that same media is also very irresponsible. All they do, especially the popular media, is report about murders and depressing things.

But we are still in love with the media—a sort of Stockholm syndrome. We are horrified sometimes, but we still can't get enough of it and hang on to it. And before you know it, you are being massaged into thinking the way the media thinks, and then you begin to believe that something that was not previously beautiful is now beautiful. Take skin colour for example. Gradually people began to say yes, dark skin is beautiful, and they have beautiful models, with Iman and others. Gradually we changed our opinion of Afro-Caribbean people and Afro-Caribbean features. These are sea changes—massive for the world—and they happened because of the media. If you ask me, women's rights happened more because of the media and not the American Bill. The same with black rights in the USA and the Jan Lokpal Bill in India, which started out as a people's movements. Think of the Nirbhaya movement after the appalling rape and physical assault of a young student on a moving bus, which eventually led to her death, and the speed at which the rapists were not only found but tried and punished. So many women are raped and killed every day. However, if the media is constantly focusing on it, then institutions pick it up.

There is a very good film called *Wag the Dog*, where the president invents a war. It's not really happening—it's happening in a Hollywood studio. Everyone says 'Oh my God, we are in danger. You better vote for the president for the next election. We don't want anyone new because he is a tough man.' You can actually help to alter people's sense of reality. We only know the media outside our observational personal presence. We only know the outside world through the media and whatever the media tells us. Like they tell us that Stephen Hawking was the greatest brain since Einstein.

It is time for you to ask yourself, which medium are you being massaged by? And which media do you massage others with? Don't think that access to the media is only to massage other people. You are doing it every day on WhatsApp, Facebook and Instagram with whatever you post. Make no mistake, you are massaging all the time.

Symbolism Hijacks the Mind

Most of us think and communicate in words, which is great. But sometimes, to make a deeper impression, we need to go beyond words into symbols, as they are more effective at communicating messages and inspiring people. I spent a large amount of time on public service campaigns and found that many times, people's minds must be open to be mentally massaged.

A picture might paint a thousand words, but a symbol can conjure a million emotions.

For example, I did an ad on the benefits of wearing helmets without showing any car accidents. The police commissioner of Mumbai called me aghast and said, 'But Mr Padamsee, you haven't told people they must wear helmets!'

I said, 'I have.'

The ad was 39 seconds long. It showed two coconuts, one with a helmet over it and another without. Then two burly men take hammers and hit the coconuts with brute force. The uncovered coconut smashes open and all the water gushes everywhere. The coconut covered by the helmet is unaffected. Then a one liner: *It's your choice. After all it's your head.*'

Now, is there really a need to spell it out or to show it?

Another film that I made about family planning was very symbolic. There's a glass jar on the table. A man's hand puts one tomato into the jar. Then he puts another tomato in and a third tomato, which comes up to the rim of the jar. He picks up the cover of the jar and he pushes it down, but it will not close properly. So, he pushes harder, and all the tomatoes turn to pulp. The camera zooms in, and it's quite a bloody scene because of the red colour of the tomatoes. That was the idea, of course. There's only one line and it's still quite well known. It is the family planning slogan, '*Ek ya do. Bas,*' or 'One or two. That's enough.'

The family planning people said, 'Are you mad? Nobody understands this ad about tomatoes.'

I said, 'OK, if you don't think so, we can test it out.'

So, we went to villages and we ran a test. The results were amazing. As much as 80 per cent of the men said, 'Yes, we know it's about family planning. If we have too many children, we won't be able to provide for them all and they will perish.'

I said, 'In what way?'

'There would be no roof over their heads, they won't get an education, they won't have food to eat, they will be destroyed in that way.'

We also asked the women.

'It definitely means don't hurt children. Just have two.'

Another said, 'If you have too many, you won't be able to share your love amongst them, or be able to nurse them when they're sick . . .' For them, it was all about not being able to nurture too many children.

We tested across seventy-seven women and eighty-five men. The results were clear, and in my favour.

I said, 'There you are, people understand symbols, but they don't understand long sentences.'

That same film was voted around the world as the most efficient use of symbolism. Children and tomatoes: people understand it, as long as it is dramatic.

So, in your life, are you just full of words? Or do you bring symbolism in so others get a deeper message? How do you show others you really care? Try symbols—you won't regret it.

Turning the Tables

Some years ago, for some mad reason, I was appointed advisor to the Cancer Society. They were doing a campaign with O & M and asked me to review it.

It was very striking. It said, 'Seven warning signs of cancer'. And then it said, 'What a pity he didn't pay any attention.' Then they had a tombstone that said, 'Rest in Peace'.

I said, 'Excuse me, why are you frightening them? It's frightening enough to have cancer. Take me. I read your ad and I say, if I do have any of these seven signs of cancer, the last thing I will do is to go to a cancer doctor. Why? Because I know I'm going to die. You are telling people—no, basically giving them—the seven signs of death! Do you think anyone will come for a check-up? They don't want to know that they are going to die. Cancer and death have now become inextricably joined.'

They understood and said, 'So what should we do?'

I answered, 'What you need to do is give them hope. You can't give them terrifying messages.'

'Yes, Mr Padamsee, but you know, we thought fear would be a great motivator.'

I said, 'No, fear is the worst motivator! A lot of people think it's a motivator, but it is not. Indira Gandhi frightened people during the Emergency, and as soon as the Emergency was over, they threw her out of office. She had the worst defeat in her life. Hitler instilled fear.'

You see, fear is a short-term adrenalin rush. A much better rush is hope. Hope is a long-term thing. People can go on hoping that one day a Dalit will have the same opportunities as a Brahmin.

So I said, 'Why don't we have a campaign based on hope? If cancer is curable, the campaign should be: "There is life after cancer and it's worth living."'

We did that, and then we got cancer patients who had survived cancer to speak. I said, 'Don't say "cancer victims"! They are conquerors! Give them a sense of self—"I am a conqueror of cancer", not "I have survived". The current main message goes to the seven signs of cancer. Instead, let's focus on getting it checked out and saying that if you've got cancer, it's treatable.'

Sell hope. It is sustainable.

Be Handsomely Audacious

Times change and emotions change with them. Fairness creams were at one time acceptable. And this is a story from back then, simply to illustrate a different point. I completely acknowledge the issues surrounding colourism—indeed, the whole purpose of this book is to get people out of that kind of old-fashioned thinking.

Emami is based in Calcutta and was then a small company of with a Rs 500-crore turnover. They were keen to get their fairness cream to be on par with or better than 'Fair and Lovely', which was the touchstone of fairness creams. It was commonly known as the 'God brand'.

Now, I was observing people around me and I noticed one day that a friend of mine kept on checking out his face. I realized something interesting: Men were also vain.

And that's when I said to Emami, 'You'll never beat them in female fairness, so why don't you try male fairness?'

Well, they all had a good laugh out of it. 'How can you talk about male fairness? Men don't want to be fair!'

And I said, 'Alright, let's run a test. Let's put up mirrors in a hundred shops and tabulate how many women enter and look in the mirror and how many men do.'

The result was amazing. In women, it was like 88 per cent and in men, a staggering 75 per cent.

The agency came up with twenty names, and we settled on 'Fair and Handsome'. We launched in Hyderabad, putting up about a hundred hoardings where we didn't talk about our product at all. They simply said, 'We don't wear bangles, so then why do we wear their cream?' or 'We don't wear a bindi. Why do we wear their cream?'

Everybody said, 'Wow, wow, wow.' There was no mention of the cream, but it set the stage. People knew it was something to do with advertising something. Then after two weeks, we launched a fairness cream for men, 'Fair and Handsome'. Just like that, it took off like a rocket. Oh, I wish I'd taken 1 per cent of the sales as commission . . . I'd have become a billionaire.

I think the brands I created are unique. They're unique because they broke the rules and changed the battlefield.

What are you doing differently to change the battlefields in your life? Which rules can you break to make a new game?

Arousing the Creative Juices to Create the Next Big Thing

I've been thinking for years about the scourge of AIDS. Every day there's an article on AIDS and it killing people, that we can't get a vaccine against it. Information has been spread: 'Don't have sex without a CONDOM'. So, the condom is your only protection against AIDS and other sexually transmitted diseases.

I was thinking about it. 'Why? If we have got the solution in our hands, why hasn't AIDS been eliminated from the world?'

Then I realized that I myself am as guilty as others of having sex occasionally without a condom. And I said, why do that? And all the men reading this know why. It is because sex without a condom is more pleasurable. That is the truth of the matter. It is not like I invented it. It is an actual natural truth. I was reminded of my eldest daughter who used to hate medicine. Why? When we were young, medicine tasted bitter.

Today, my second daughter happily glugs down a vitamin tonic. I asked myself why does she glug it down when my eldest daughter used to hate it? Then I realized that the Americans had made all vitamin tonics taste nice. *There was something that appealed to people and therefore made them desire it.* So, if you can make the condom desirable to men, they would start putting it on.

So why can't we invent a condom which gives you a better sensation of sex than without a condom?

It sounds ridiculous—what am I saying? Well, if it can happen with medicine, it can happen with condoms. It can happen with so many things—just make it desirable. And I put this idea across to the then prime minister. He said, 'It sounds like a very good idea.'

He then picked up the phone and spoke to the department of biotechnology, who spoke to IIT Bombay, where I was on the advisory board, and said, 'Work with it.'

One of the professors there has already invented, if you like, a kind of 'pleasurable gel' which actually gives you a full-fledged . . . well, I presume you're all adults here, a full-fledged erection. Now, we are working on how to have the inner coating of the condom that we produce made of this substance. That's a slightly more technical problem. And once that is out, they're going to try, and if it succeeds, it means that in the end, sex with a condom . . . gentlemen, good news coming your way . . . sex with a condom will be more pleasurable than sex without a condom.

It's a little idea.

Fire was a little idea.

The wheel was a little idea, but see what it has done? The condom isn't a big idea like splitting the atom, but it can save lives that are being lost to AIDS, and it can also accelerate the one thing that this country needs. Besides food, what does this country need among the 80 per cent who are in the small towns and villages? It needs population control. I've worked on many population control task forces and they have all failed. 'Vasectomy'—as you know, Sanjay Gandhi made that a dirty word. And 'condom'— men are just not interested. Because they say, 'Every time I have to put this on. Why can't I use it once and that's enough? Then I should be free . . .' We can't do that, so this could also help in family planning in countries like India and other overpopulated places like Indonesia. In Africa, in certain countries and states, the population has been cut by 25 per cent just due to AIDS. So, what I'm saying is that if this succeeds, we've got a real breakthrough.

Little ideas can spark big changes. I remember how I began to share a handwritten slogan at work every week or so. People loved them. We had this one tough guy who was a client services controller. I talked to him, and told him be softer and kinder, but it wasn't in his DNA. So, I wrote a little line—just three words: *'Enthuse don't enforce.'*

He said, 'AP, I am not enforcing. I'm just telling them they must do it the right way.' You can see that the way he was talking was already the wrong way.

I said, 'Can you work out three or four ways to put it to them, enthusiastically? We will motivate them to do it rather than command.'

That suddenly became my motto. And I found that has changed my whole attitude.

Go back to the drawing board and think about creating a little idea that can enthuse people's thinking.

Conclusion: Commandeer Your Mind, Be the Change Agent

I'm hoping that this book is already keeping your brain on its toes.

I like this idea of you all being change agents, AP's APs if you will. You could be Alyque Padamsee's agent provocateurs by using these principles in your everyday life. You know, people who come to me always leave buzzing with ideas. They say, 'Oh wow, you give me such a novel perspective. Now I look at the situation differently!'

That's what an agent provocateur does. Just by talking to you, or showing you something, s/he changes your view of it. So come on, change the battlefields in your life and start living more fully. And watch how you grow!

Completing the Incomplete . . . Alyque Style

R. Gopalakrishnan
Former Director, Tata Sons, and Vice Chairman, HLL

I once asked David Ogilvy whether he still believed in his eponymous statement, 'If you have nothing to say, sing it.' He affirmed his view and we left it at that.

After some weeks, without referring to the Ogilvy interaction, I engaged with Alyque on the effectiveness of jingles. He stared at me and said, 'Have you heard about the Zeigarnik effect?'

Bluma Zeigarnik, a Ukrainian psychologist, published a paper in 1927, mentioning that when a task or message is complete, there is a tendency to forget about it. When the message or task is incomplete, then one tends to remember it.

For example, don't railway catering waiters always remember to collect money from those who have not yet paid? In the same way, listeners complete popular jingles in their mind, could I not understand? He went on to hum:

Tanduroosti ki raksha karta hai Lifebuoy, what follows?

'Washing powder Nirma, what follows?'

Extracting the Essence

- Newspapers have compartmentalized our lives.
- The emotional retina is your best way to sales.
- A picture really can convey a thousand words, but a symbol conjures up a million emotions.
- Hope is a more productive sell than fear.
- If you don't become a change agent, then who will?

Hijacking Your Mind—Points for You to Ponder

- Where are you selling in a productive way? How can you think about it differently?
- What boring areas of your life can you make exciting?
- How are you creating change?

7

School versus Edutainment

Igniting the Internal Combustion Engine

About forty years ago, I said, 'What I do is edutainment.'

And I still stand by it. My purpose is to educate in an entertaining way.

This idea owes its life to my school days. I realized then that, unless a teacher was entertaining, I couldn't learn. Of course, most of them at that time (and as I understand, today) were not entertaining at all. And that made me totally disinterested in education.

However, I would still go home to read books. That was because my sister, Jerry, enthused me. She understood my nature and found books that she knew I would like. She didn't just hand them to me though. She would tell me just enough of the story to pique my curiosity and make the book come alive in my mind. And then I would have no option but to read it to find out more. For instance, she introduced me to the 'Just William' series of books by Richmal Crompton. They were about a schoolboy, like me at the time, and were absolutely hysterical! After devouring those, she gave me Guy de Maupassant, followed by Hector Hugh

Munro, better known as Saki. Books speak to us in a way that little else can.

From there on, I was unstoppable. Jerry had unleashed a thirst within me which took me away from boring old school. I would read anything and everything that interested me, whether it was age-appropriate or not. I moved on to—wait for it—Richard von Krafft-Ebing at an exceedingly early age. You may know that he is the man who investigated deviant sexual behaviour, so I knew all about sexual aberrations by the time I was twelve. I never practised them, but I always thought, later in life, you never know—it might come in useful (!).

I read books on philosophy, and one of my brothers, Bobby, was particularly in love with books on Greek and Roman mythology. So outside of dull school, I was brought up on Perseus, Hercules and all the great mythical figures of Rome, fire-breathing dragons and other stuff like that. All this inflamed my imagination, lit by a combustion of written words on a page and my ever-working brain. Some of my dreams used to be with these characters—not with Superman or Batman, but with the Gorgons, who could turn men into stone.

Years later, the magic from Roman and Greek myths would influence both my advertising and theatre. People like the Liril girl—she's really a water sprite. She prances about in the water and she's, in a sense, magical. The MRF Man is very like Hercules. He's got these bulging muscles and is holding up a heavy tyre, and it's known as the 'tyre with muscle', which is to do with strength. In *Legend of Lovers*, Shazahn disappears from lying on a bed and suddenly reappears at the door. These myths influenced my thinking and imagination.

The right kind of books ignite something deep inside. Our internal spirit is mystical and magical, and the right kind of education sets it on fire.

But I never found class interesting when they were simply reeling off a list of facts or telling me things. That did not ignite me.

ALYQUEISM: Have you noticed how many American expressions are visual? 'Hit the ground running', 'Keep your eyes peeled' . . . The power of the visual is so strong, it's amazing.

Now, how can we bring visual stimulation to the classroom?

Rules at School Followed the Rulers

Thou hast most traitorously corrupted the youth of the realm in erecting a grammar-school.

—*Henry VI*, Part 2, Act IV, Scene VII

For years, education in this country and almost all over the world was about rote learning. And unfortunately, Britain was in India during the Victorian period. If Britain had been our rulers after the Beatles, just imagine how different life could have been. The Beatles generation disrupted the culture of Britain completely. It was an exciting time over there, where people were doing mad things that didn't have logic. No linear thinking, but squiggly thinking, all over the place. If post-Beatles Britain had ruled India, I think India would have been quite a different place. We actually had Britain ruling over us during its worst period, at its most conventional, with, 'Don't answer back. Little boys should be silent and only speak when they are spoken to.' And as for little girls . . .

We have continued in this trap, this time worshipping the false gods of education. We are still handcuffed to the old system. Education here in India is for the teacher to dictate, no questions asked. A lot has changed abroad, which I must say is very good, but most of what is being taught in Indian schools is unfortunately still very much by rote, where you learn by heart, faithfully reproduce in the examination and you pass to get your degree. Do you really want a degree that says you are nothing more than a robot?

Garbage in, garbage out? I mean look at History—these poor kids today have to learn all these dates and reel them off in the exam. They get marks for getting the dates right. BUT WHO CARES ABOUT THE DATE if they don't understand the crux of *why the war was fought*, or the significance of the action? History is not about dates; history says it was thanks to a man like Gandhiji that we got our independence through non-violence, which everyone said was impossible. Now how did we do that? Can we bring that teaching in?

In Xavier's College, where I was on the advisory committee, I said to the Principal, 'Look, one of the main problems that students face is the teaching method.'

He said, 'What do you mean by that?'

I said, 'When I was in college, and I think even until today, most professors tend to dictate knowledge, not teach it. And it doesn't work for the students. The professors have a textbook with the syllabus and literally force it down the students' throat with no creativity. I think that's wrong. I think if they could make the students fall in love with the subject, the students would educate themselves. That's the job of a teacher: not to *tell* the student, but *to tempt the student to fall in love with the subject.*'

I am saying education is for *the learner to learn* and not for the teacher to teach. It's for the teacher to *enthuse*, and it's for the learner to be enthusiastic enough to be able to learn on their own. That's what education is all about.

Falling in Love with Learning

Two of my favourite examples of this are not works that I've created, like advertising campaigns, but incidents that I have actually witnessed. My daughter, Shazahn, like all my children, was always failing at Hindi, and I asked myself, 'How do I make her fall in love with Hindi?'

It was a different language with a totally different script, and I think behind all that was the unspoken prejudice that it was a language spoken by the household help. She and her friends never spoke to other friends or relatives in Hindi, only to servants. In a sense, the Hindi language ended up getting a bad reputation because of this.

I asked myself, 'How can we make her fall in love with Hindi when she finds it very difficult and not hip or trendy in the slightest?'

After much pondering, in true AP fashion, I actioned an experiment. I asked all the mothers in the surrounding neighbourhood in the carpool, 'Is your daughter having problems with Hindi?'

Goodness, they groaned and said, 'Yes, my God, it's a nightmare. How on earth are any of them going to pass the exam?'

So, I said, 'I've got an idea. I'm going to start a trendy club at home, the Hindi club. We can come up with a snazzy name for it later. I'll get a good friend of mine who is a theatre actor to give me an upcoming actor. I will pay him to come twice a week to my house. I want him to teach these five kids three things: one, a Hindi joke; two, a Hindi song and three, to be able to do an improvisation in Hindi. But the improvisation should be something funny.'

It was the Hindi Hijack.

When the girls first found out, they thought, 'Oh God, it's in Hindi.' But when they heard the first Hindi joke, it was like an infection—really, it was like they had caught some kind of disease. The next day they went to school and told the joke in Hindi to their friends. Now, many of their friends were very fluent in Hindi. The friends laughed, and the girls were thrilled. The next time the guy came, they said, 'Hey, teach us another joke because our friends loved it and we've become very popular with them.'

Motivation at work! They were enthused.

The second was a song. They learned a popular Hindi song and its meaning. One of the girls told me that the next time relatives came over, there was the usual, 'My *beti* (daughter) can sing a song.' The mother said, 'Go on beti, sing the song for them.' She sang and everyone clapped, so of course she felt exceptionally good.

The third one was just gaining familiarity with being able to improvise. However, you have to have enough vocabulary and a little command of the language to do this. They worked at it and within weeks they were imitating actors and serials in full gusto.

I would say they fell in love with Hindi and also began to see how useful it was to have the Hindi language in their lives. They could bargain better with the traders in Bandra, that was for sure!

The second example I can give about education is with my son, Quasar, who was failing at maths with alarming regularity. We got a tutor for him, and Dolly was extremely strict. She told him, 'You can't play cricket until you finish your homework.'

Did it work? Despite his love for cricket, NO! Every day he would start his homework but never finish it, so he couldn't play cricket at all. He continued to fail at maths. I realized we had to take a different approach. I said to Dolly, 'Look, the time for promotion to the next class is coming at the end of the year. If he fails, his promotion goes.' She said, 'Yes, I've been telling him that he'll fail.'

I said, 'Do you mind if I take over?'

Dolly, exasperated with both father and son, said, 'Oh alright, you think you know everything. Let's see if you can work your magic on him.'

I took Q out for an ice cream. I said, 'Beta, you like making new friends?'

He gulped his ice cream down happily and said, 'I love making new friends.'

I just nodded, saying, 'You'll be making a lot of new friends very soon—that's so exciting.'

And it was that simple. I didn't say that he would fail. Never once did I use the word 'fail' because that is demotivating.

He said, 'How Dad, tell me how?'

'Well, if your maths doesn't go well, you won't be promoted. And then you'll make a lot of new friends as the boys in the junior class will come up to your class, and you will be the most senior of all of them. So you see, you'll have lots of new friends.'

But then it hit him that he'd lose all his old friends. He began to study maths because it was *a need for him*. It was no longer Dad or Mum saying, 'Do your homework.'

It became personal. He could see the benefit immediately, and that was his motivation.

It's the same at work when bosses say, 'Work harder.'

You think, 'Well, why should I work harder when I'm getting the same salary?' But as soon as you give them a motivation, it changes everything.

Quasar's Tryst with Edutainment

Quasar Padamsee
Artistic Director, QTP Entertainment Pvt. Ltd

None of us Padamsee kids were interested in formal education, and Dad was always trying to solve this! He was brilliant at inverting the conversation. He told me 'I know you don't like maths, but I promise, if you become good at it, you'll enjoy it.'

And he was right.

I decided to give it a go and worked incredibly hard with my tutor in maths. And I ended up doing really well in the next maths test. And that made me feel so good! No surprise that I ended up getting better at it, and even carried on for 11th and 12th. That was all down to Dad's initial idea of getting me to do the opposite of what I wanted.

Vandana keeps reminding me that the word 'education' comes from 'educos', which means 'to bring out that which is within'. And I think we have forgotten that. It is not about cramming notes. The way we teach currently ensures our knowledge just goes into cold storage, never to see the light of day in our heads. True education is about getting a strong foundation in many areas, so that we can bring it out and integrate it with other knowledge, to get better results.

Why do you think that company boards are always looking for non-executive directors who have knowledge and experience different from the rest of the board? It is because they are looking for diversity of ideas. Yes, experience can give that to you, but it starts with what we learn at school and at home. The more we are taught to be enthused about learning, the more we are likely to appreciate learning later in our careers. I think the wide variety of books I was exposed to at an early age have contributed to me having multiple careers and doing well in all of them.

Think about the example that I gave in Chapter 5 about C?Os. IIT Bombay wanted me on board because I thought in a different way than the rest of those engineers. I brought a fresh outlook on what they were aiming to do. I helped them think out of the box. That was, in a way, edutaining them.

Hindi Hijack—The Prequel!

Sharon Prabhakar
Corporate Trainer, Theatre Actress and Singer

Alyque had a wonderful gut instinct to discover and bring out the USP in somebody. As an Anglo-Indian, I did not speak Hindi, and I had only worked in English music and acting. I don't know from where he got the idea, but Alyque came to me one day and said, 'Look at the world of Hindi music, Hindi drama and Hindi acting. It's time for you to be there.'

At that time, the idea of doing anything Hindi sounded Greek to me, but a little voice inside me said yes. My journey into the exciting world of languages began. It was a lot of hard work, but I discovered that I was ready for it. Alyque said, 'I don't want you to learn words, I don't want you to learn a script or mug poems. I want you to start thinking in the language.' Now that for me was a huge 'Aha!' moment. We found a Hindi play.

Alyque is like a camel—he puts his foot in it and then takes over the whole tent! He suddenly said, 'It has to be a two-person play.' So there we were, putting together this zany comedy in Hindi. That was my initiation into not only the world of thinking in Hindi but also broadening my own horizons. He then insisted I had to learn about Hindi and put me on a journey of eight years with a guru mastering the Patiala Gharana. I studied and sang. These were the two foundations to the rest of my life. Both these things, speaking and singing in Hindi, manifested into different forms or challenges. It meant that I could do courses and compering in Hindi—even do comedy sketches!

Now I find I don't think in English anymore, I think in Hindi! I tend to start off in English and then completely automatically slip into Hindi. My mind was hijacked by my love for Hindi and the world that opened up for me. I thank him for this as I would have been living my life in a narrow little box and waiting for walls to expand. Walls don't expand. You expand. Ideas expand. Ambitions expand. So destroy the walls.

Edutainment through Proverbs

One part of my childhood that I am quite grateful for is the time I spent at Miss Murphy's school. I was extremely young at the time, but this is where, quite honestly, I learnt the principles of life. And really, it was the start of understanding edutainment for me. Because she brought education to life. How?

Visual stimulation through proverbs.

It's amazing how many of us are brought up on proverbs—I certainly know I was. Miss Murphy, who was a grand old Irish woman, was always quoting 'a stitch in time'. Then she would explain what it meant. She would say, 'If you get it done today, then you can do something else with your time tomorrow. Why procrastinate?' You could literally imagine someone stitching a hole up so that it would not get worse in the next few days, because if it did, it might become too big to fix. I could literally SEE the proverb in my head. And even though, at that age, I had no clue what procrastination was, I got the gist of it.

Miss Murphy had a fantastic vocabulary, and that's how my brother Bobby got involved in literature and the theatre. Bobby was the one I would credit for our generation falling in love with theatre.

Back to Miss Murphy. Miss Murphy insisted that 'honesty is the best policy'. She didn't mean honesty just in money, but honesty in thinking. That your honesty in thinking and your attitude towards life should be an honest one. For example, don't cheat and don't tell lies because you want to get away with something—it will always come back to haunt you. That was very important.

The proverb that impressed me the most and I think has been the central to my life is linked to the English writer Frederick Maryat and from *The Children of the New Forest*. It is, of course, 'If at first you don't succeed, try, and try again.'[1] I learnt these proverbs, and as I would hear these little nuggets, I was very fond of collecting them. What I loved about proverbs and quotations was that they really opened your eyes to principles of living in a very entertaining, relatable way.

For instance, Kennedy had a wonderful way of saying, 'Don't think you're born to only satisfy yourself.' And that's why he started the Peace Corps. That's what good phrases, proverbs and teachers do: they stir something inside of you and set you on fire.

Find Your Passion

Do you realize that anyone coming into the workforce today will be working for at least six decades of their life?

That is an astounding length of time. When we were young, we thought we would work until sixty and then retire. No one ever thought we would work for so many more years. Do you really think you will be doing the same thing for all those six decades?

No.

And that is why we need a broader definition of what education is. It is not just what you learn at school or the skills for the workplace. It includes how you build yourself into an all-rounder, so you can do anything that you want to. I would also say that for anyone, not just millennials: when you really fall in love with something, you suddenly realize who you are *internally*. That's what real education does to you. It ignites a passion! And the sooner you find your passion in life, the better. But do not give up if you can't find it immediately. When it comes, it hits you for a six and you are never the same again.

'But Alyque, that's easy to say. But how do I find my passion?' I hear some of you asking. The answer is simple.

Be consistently curious and open about life. And allow life to happen to you. Amidst all of this, you will find your passion, mark my words.

Curiosity Did Not Kill the Cat

I get quite annoyed with this proverb, as it is not entirely accurate. Shakespeare had it right in *Much Ado About Nothing*, where Claudio says to Benedick, 'What, courage, man! What though *care killed a cat*? Thou hast mettle enough in thee to kill care.' In this instance, care meant worries. So Shakespeare was saying worrisome thoughts would kill you. That is not at all the same as curiosity! I wouldn't be surprised if those religious zealots of times gone by changed the phrase to get people to stay in line and not question religion too much! Anyway, I say, 'Curiosity inspired the cat', and that has proven true throughout my life. Curiosity is the best form of edutainment anywhere.

Honestly, if you just keep your eyes wide open and go explore different areas, you will somehow stumble upon your passion. I'll give you an example. I remember my brother, Chotu, being a complete stud in his early days. To him, life was rich parents, going out every night, drinking and coming back at four in the morning. In short, he did practically nothing. When he was seventeen and I was eighteen, we went to London together, where I got involved in looking for an education in law, while simultaneously working in theatre in the evenings. Chotu? Well, erm, I don't remember him doing much! While he lounged around, I was busy trying to fulfil my mother's dream of me becoming a lawyer. I went to Lincoln Inns Fields in London, where I was told that I would have to work in the evenings and take client briefs. That interfered with theatre rehearsals for me, so that was where my mother's dreams ended. And it is exactly where I realized that my passion was theatre, so I ended up joining the Royal Academy of Dramatic Art (RADA). Chotu, on the other hand, chilled, then did a course at St Martin's School of Art. When I finished RADA, he came back to India with me. I remember he did absolutely nothing again, until he became curious about planes. Two years later, he was taking flying lessons, which he found very glamorous. He was gung-ho about flying and so decided to join the RAF. So, he went to London on his own and applied to be a fighter pilot.

They told him, 'It's all very well that you have the pilot's licence, but for us, you need to have an "A" licence.'

He asked, 'How do I get that?'

They then told him he would have to sign a form and be commissioned for ten years.

Well, Chotu was not willing to sign up for that length of time, so gave up on that idea.

As the rest of us were all so involved in theatre, a little while later, he chose to take up a side course, in theatre. And part of the theatre training was . . . architecture.

Why was it so important for the theatre?

Well, it is important to think about what kinds of theatres there are—the size, the acoustics, the design. Think about it—all round the world we have these wonderful buildings dedicated to theatre, from the Globe Theatre in Stratford Upon Avon to Palladio's Teatro Olimpico in Vincenza, Italy. For heaven's sake, India had the most magnificent theatres, but unfortunately through history, they have been demolished. Anyway, just like that, Chotu fell in love with architecture. On his own he decided to join the Architectural Association, which at that time was the biggest and the best. After his first year of studying, he got a scholarship and he went on to become the dean of several colleges of architecture, both globally and in India, totally in love with architecture. Phew! He got there.

The moral of this story is that it sometimes takes ten or twelve attempts to find your passion, and that's OK. Keep looking. As the proverb goes, 'If at first you don't succeed, try and try again.' Keep going until you find your passion. It will keep you entertained for as long as you are on this planet.

Learning as A Way of Life

I realize as I look back at the years that while school was boring because of the rote learning, I ended up just observing everything that was going on around me and learning from that. It's a kind of life-long learning that has served me well over the years. And because it doesn't feel like school, I am willing to do it over and over again.

Conclusion

Edutainment and enlightened entertainment—that's what new age education should be about. You're enlightening the students in an entertaining way. In fact, we should invent a new category. This book is not self-help. This book should not be considered a business book but should be in this category of enlightened entertainment that hasn't been created yet. Well, now it can be!

I don't think we should underestimate the importance of bringing education to life. So many breakthroughs happen at the intersection of two disparate fields. You've got technology and you've got people and the interaction between the two is going to change the future. It's important to have people who understand technology but also people who are creative and can work out different uses for that technology.

Postscript: Qualifications

Perhaps it is time to award different qualifications. Why do we not award people for the skills that they have picked up during their lives? Their passions and deep interests? Why do you have to have a degree from a recognized place for it to be considered 'real'? Is my experience not real? I believe I should receive a PhD in

Orson Welles and Shakespeare. Vandana, my collaborator, most certainly has a PhD in Alyque Padamsee thinking and diplomas in networking and the understanding of many business people. We need to rethink education big time.

Every day with Alyque was like going to university. And graduating!
—Bugs Bhargava, Actor and Director

Extracting the Essence

» Edutainment is the way to fall in love with lifelong learning.
» If we don't live in Victorian England anymore, why the hell are we subjecting our kids to it in the classroom?
» Curiosity made the cat find her passion (probably in her ninth life).
» Different qualifications should be awarded in the future.

Hijacking Your Mind—Points for You to Ponder

» Think about a subject you hated. Now think about the teacher. Is there a connection?
» How can you make your employees or your kids learn in a more fun manner?
» How do you make learning fun for you?
» To whom can you award an alternative qualification and why would you do it? What would you award yourself?

8

Repaying the Accident of Birth

Bonus Babies

Oh You, Who Have Everything . . .

Wow. Lucky you. You are one of the luckiest people in the world. Yes, I am talking to you, the one reading this book. Have you ever realized just how lucky you are?

'I beg your pardon?' I hear you say. 'You have no idea about my life, Alyque—the troubles I have been through and the sorrows I have faced. How dare you call me lucky? You don't know me.'

Well, excuse me for being presumptuous, but there is an exceptionally good reason if I am being that way. If you have the ability to read this book, it means you are somewhat educated. If you have the ability to buy this book or read a ripped off copy of it online (shame on you), then you have money, either to purchase the book or to have a mobile phone, Kindle or computer.

And that puts you in the top 1 per cent of the global population. You are not one of the two-thirds of the population on earth that live on less than $10 a day. Or one of the 10 per cent that live on less than $1 a day. You are not being trafficked for sex or begging on the sides of the street. I doubt you are living in inhospitable, unbearable conditions. And I bet you have access to decent drinking water, as well as three meals a day, should you want them.

So I say again, lucky you.

I was lucky enough to be born into a rich family. We had two chauffeur-driven cars. My father owned ten buildings and I didn't have to take up a job. Imagine that, I never had to work until I was twenty-three or twenty-four. There was no pressure to take up my father's business. I could do what I liked. I was so lucky that I had been born into this house and have had all these privileges . . .

We are blind to what we've already been given.

And here I am, getting old. It makes me think more and it makes me angrier. Every time I pass a slum or hear about someone poor committing suicide, like farmers, it is like a hammer that hits me over the head: 'Oh my God, thank God I wasn't born into a farming family.'

Seeing people around me in our under-developed India really kills me. We have over 150 million children undernourished and starving, who are, in all honesty, going to die. And therefore, doesn't it become kind of a moral responsibility for us to do something? Would you help people if you could? I'm not necessarily saying starve your children and give to others. However, if you have three meals a day, a roof over your head, you go on holiday regularly, you enjoy life a limited amount, then you should be saying, 'How can I help other people?' People like you must realize you're what I call 'bonus babies'. Actually, I think you do know, but you perhaps haven't truly realized the benefit you are getting in life. Most people just take it as God's gift to them. For example, I never realized how I had been born into a lot of richness, whether in terms of money, relationships or belonging.

So yes, you there reading this are in fact a 'bonus baby'. You have an unfair advantage—you have had a silver spoon dangling out of your mouth from the day you were born. I know you know this. But I don't want it in the back of your mind. I want to bring it slap-bang into the front!

If each individual in the world can, in some way, stop thinking about themselves and look at the bigger picture, we will collectively change the world. Yes, I know you have this worry and that worry. Perhaps the bills are getting higher and he or she in your life is giving you a hard time. But can YOU begin to see how you're still lucky, because you were given the advantages that others have not been given? And are you doing anything about that?

> *ALYQUEISM: Do you realize that most of us reading this book are just sleepwalking through life?*

Exercising the Licence to Swindle

I have met many of the type that say, 'Padamsee Sahib, *maine pehle janam main bahut acha kiya. Is liye is janam main humko* reward *mila.*' That is, 'I must have done something really good in my last life and that is why I got a reward in this life.' But this rebirth thing or the seven lives is one of the biggest cons I've ever heard. People love it because it absolves them of all responsibility. 'Why did you do that to that man?' He replies, 'Because in a previous life he must've done it to me, so I'm allowed to do it.'

What a licence to swindle.

How long will we use these ideas to allow ourselves to get away with turning a blind eye to the suffering of others? Or let's put it another way: if you have the opportunity to stop someone else's suffering, why aren't you doing it? You could be putting in some credits for your next life too! At the same time, perhaps he or she is not meant to suffer in this life; perhaps you are *supposed* to do something to help him or her.

Whichever way you look at it, why not act on it, rather than swindling others by peddling prehistoric thoughts?

Great Leaders—What a Bonus!

What unifies people is a great spirit. Gandhi unified people, poor and rich, with the idea of peace. He said, 'Non-violence is the greatest force at the disposal of mankind. It is mightier than the mightiest weapon of destruction devised by the ingenuity of man.' And Nelson Mandela said, 'Men of peace must not think about retribution or recriminations. Courageous people do not fear forgiving, for the sake of peace.'[1] Remember they had both been through a lot personally and seen people close to them attacked and murdered. They had seen their nations ravaged and pillaged. They had seen injustice at the highest levels. Yet they had it in their hearts to let go of the past, to move on.

Which is why we have the world we have today.

So how can the new generation begin to say, every day when they get up, 'I'm so lucky.'

Gandhi was a man who said, 'I am going to defy the British.' And he was prepared to go to jail for picking up a handful of salt as he did on the Dandi march. Remember what led up to this momentous event. The British Salt Act of 1882 prohibited Indians from collecting or selling salt. How ridiculous is that? (Well, not so ridiculous if you look at the rules we are still following today in this book!) So Indians were required to pay a heavy salt tax to buy from the British. Gandhi wrote to Viceroy Irwin, telling him that they would start making salt. Gandhi then planned to walk from Sabarmati Ashram to Dandi, on the Arabian Sea, where he and his followers would make salt. Now, when Gandhi started that yatra out there, he had about a hundred followers. But as he went along, more and more people joined him. Rich people, poor people . . . they joined because they believed in his idea that we could win our independence without violence. It was an idea bigger than anything of its time. And even Einstein said, 'Generations to come will scarce believe that such a one as this ever in flesh and blood walked upon this Earth . . . We should strive to do things in his spirit: not to use violence in fighting for our cause, but by non-participation in anything you believe is evil.'[2]

I understand that the British MP William Wilberforce spoke out against slavery in 1789. He was adamant to not just change the law, but change people's minds about slavery. He said America should not have slaves, and then it was taken up in the parliament. He inspired Abraham Lincoln. Before the abolition of slavery in both countries, people said, 'What's wrong with slavery? We're feeding them and giving them everything but money and an education.' These are radical ideas that changed nations and made life better for millions across the world.

How can you be a modern-day unifier? I don't mean that you need to build a movement on the scale that Gandhi did (although I would be happy if you did!). But can you stand up for those who don't have the same 'bonus' as you? And get others to do it too?

Repaying the Silver Spoon: Akanksha

I want to recount one of my favourite stories to illustrate this point. Those of you who remember BBC's 'Listen with Mother' will know this first line: 'Are you sitting comfortably? Then we'll begin.'

Once upon a time, there was a young student from St Xavier's College in Mumbai. She used to walk past a slum, every day, on her way to college with friends. All the skinny, half-clothed children would be playing constantly. One day, she asked one of her friends, 'Why aren't those children in school?'

The others shrugged their shoulders.

The first persisted, 'Why don't we go to find out?'

And so she did. She found out the children were not in school because they were not accepted by the schools. Well, this upset her immensely. And she decided to do something about it. That female college student had very few financial resources with her. But she had two resources in abundance:

The WILL. And the TIME.

And, therefore, she decided that *she* would educate those children in English. So she went to the parents of these children in the slums and told the parents what she was planning to do. One of the mothers said, 'What a wonderful idea.'

However, the father said, 'Over my dead body. Those children are earning money. I have seven children and I can't afford to feed seven children unless they contribute towards our welfare.'

The college student ignored the fathers and listened to the mothers. But there was a problem. Where would she teach the slum kids?

So, she went to the Holy Name High School in Colaba. She got an appointment with the principal and asked, 'Would you be prepared to lend one of your classrooms in the school in the evening? To educate some children?'

(I think) the principal said, 'Slum children? They would bring disease.' She was disheartened a little, but the slum children's mothers were very keen. They said that they would see to it that the children were all cleaned up.

She went back to the principal and tried again.

Now the principal had reflected on his previous answer. Being a Christian (see, sometimes religion can be helpful!), the principal said, 'Let's give it a try because somewhere inside, I love the idea.'

The college student went on to the next problem: how does she get the children to the school, if they don't have money to take buses? So she went to the bus owner of school buses and told them that the principal had agreed to them using the school. She asked, 'Would you be willing to lend your buses?'

'Yes.'

'Would you pay for the petrol?' she asked.

'Yes. This will be my own contribution to these children,' said the driver.

Akanksha[3] the organization was born. Almost three decades later, we are living in the happily-ever-after, where they now have over fifty after-school centres. They support over 2,000 children with an education that they otherwise would not have had. Their mission is to build the largest network of innovative schools that empower children to maximize their potential and influence systemic reform. They are now sharing their model and practices with the government and have spoken at many international conferences.

And that's the true story of how 'bonus baby', the amazing Shaheen Mistri, started Akanksha, one of the most outstanding NGOs in the world. They have expanded tremendously thanks to the generosity of other 'bonus babies' around the world who are inspired by their work, and if we are honest, have a bit of a guilt complex about being a 'bonus baby'. They have also inspired many others to support those who have not been supported for generations.

Is that 'the happily ever after' of the story?

Of course not!

Not content with building Akanksha, Shaheen Mistri felt she needed to increase the dialogue around the issue of educational inequity across India and do something practical about it. She met Wendy Kopp, who founded an organization called Teach for America. She approached brilliant people like Anu Aga and Meher Pudumjee, who helped her create Teach for India[4] (TFI), which is about leadership in education. TFI now has over 900 fellows working in classrooms and creating change themselves.

Wow! How absolutely inspirational.

It is happening everywhere. Vandana tells me about the wonderful work that Lighthouse Communities Foundation (LCF, earlier Pune City Connect) does. This enterprising group of bonus babies, including Dr Ganesh Natarajan (founder and chairman, 5F World), realized they have had it easy and wanted to make the world easier for others. Lighthouse Communities is a pioneering model for social transformation that enables the government, non-profits, corporates, citizens—basically anyone—to come together and contribute to social development in Pune. She talks animatedly about their 'Lighthouse' project, where thousands of youths have been trained and provided a safe space to work on their skills. Over 70 per cent have studied only up to Grade 12 or below, and all of them are from low-income communities. They go on to get jobs through the training.

You know, Lighthouse Communities also maps every student who enrols with a view to ensuring that a minimum of 20 per cent households in each of the 500+ slum communities in Pune experience the Lighthouse programme. They are also finding a way to ensure that there is one person in every slum dwelling who is digitally literate. This helps the whole family get the benefits of being digital, whether it is access to information or rewards through the internet.

LCF 'bonus babies' are giving their time and effort back to those who need it.

Another organization that I have great admiration for (in fact, quite independently, Vandana does too—she is a global trustee of theirs) is Common Purpose (CP). It was set up by another 'bonus baby', the feisty Julia Middleton. Julia was brought up around the world as her father was a diplomat, so she had first-hand experience of how different people were, but how similar we all were too. Yet they did not acknowledge their similarities or how they could help each other, because they were stuck in conventional silos. They didn't realize that by dissolving those boundaries between them, they would be able to solve private and public sector challenges. As CP says, 'We live in a world full of complex problems. These problems cross boundaries. Yet most leaders do not.' I immediately resonated with her and CP's vision of bringing different sectors together to create a better understanding to solve complex problems. Having worked with Chandrababu Naidu in Andhra Pradesh and having tried to work with Bal Thackeray in Bombay, I always felt that there was scope for deeper dialogue. *You know, nothing comes from working against the system, however rotten it is. You have to have the ability to bring the system to your side, if you want to get anything done. If you spend time pointing fingers or stand on the sidelines and throw stones at the politicians and governments, what will that achieve?*

CP is one of the few organizations, I feel, that understands the importance of civic engagement to deepen democracy. They see the need for deeper dialogue and like me, don't shy away from it. If any of you have heard Julia speak, you will know what I mean!

It is important to work from within the system and that means with the people *within* the system. But it only works if you bring the three sectors of not-for-profits, government and private enterprises together. I've been invited many times to be the CP keynote speaker when they've brought people from all over the world together, to cross boundaries. They give them challenges and all sorts of real-world problems to work together and appreciate each other. It's honestly the kind of education that should be provided in schools and universities, which would actually be useful in life. Where are we taught at school how to get along with people and how to look at different perspectives? Vandana tells me her first CP programme in 2011 had forty young leaders chosen for a UK and Indian prime minister joint-initiative called Disha. They had to come up with a way to bring heart surgery down to under a $1000! Vandana said at first she had no interest in it, as she wasn't a medic and didn't think she could contribute. But when she worked with the other enterprising leaders, they all got involved and excited. She was horrified to see how much medical companies were charging for stents and realized this was an area where something could be done. Years later, and unrelated, Advocate Birender Sangwan[5] brought his case to the Indian government and succeeded in getting the price of stents reduced drastically. She and the others came up with some fantastic ideas which were showcased to Dr Devi Shetty, no less.

Thirty years and some 90,000 alumni later, CP has changed lives across the world by getting people to be better, more inclusive leaders. They run the most marvellous programmes, where they get individuals to really question who they are 'being' in the world and who they are working with. The current CEO, Adirupa Sengupta, is taking Julia's work to new heights. Here in India, the theatre actress Munira Sen has been working at promoting Common Purpose's work, to create a common ground of equality and inclusiveness. Ah, what bonus babies they all are.

Now let's get back to the rest of us.

We are far too self-centred. We're always obsessing about 'what I'm going to do next' or 'how I can make more money'. I want to ask you, are we introspecting at all?

Are we questioning the fact that one of the things that makes us who we are is not our education, but our birth into a family that gave us three meals a day and vacations twice a year? Questioning that fact is the key, not just the fact that we have an education. Thanks to Akanksha, those slum children have been given a chance. But there are still so many that have not been given a chance.

I want to know what the baby in the slum will grow into, if it is given a chance by a 'bonus baby' like you or me.

'Bonus Baby' Leads to Bonus Feelings

So, what does 'lending a helping hand' do for you, internally?

I can't speak for you. But I can speak for myself. Acknowledging that I am a 'bonus baby' and then choosing to help others who are not has given me two things. One is a heightened individual sense of self: I was doing something that I had only talked about in my dreams and now I'm actually practising it in real life. And the second thing is that I am looking after someone who is not a blood relative, and I feel good about myself for doing that.

Feeling good about yourself is an especially important part of being a good human being. I know a lot of people who do things, but they do it grudgingly, more out of obligation than anything else. But everyone loves to get a sense of satisfaction—in fact, most thrive on it. This is the best satisfaction I have ever felt. To tell you the truth, it has made my life so much more meaningful.

Mira Savara, Phd (ex-head of research at BBC World Service Trust, worked with FREA in the 1970s), recalls:

I was working with the NGO Front for Rapid Economic Advancement in 1972. It had been set up by a group of engineering students from IIT Bombay. Its main programme was to take technical students to work on projects in Gramdan villages all over India to use their skills on development issues. One year we were running a big drought programme, and we decided we wanted to do a fundraiser and create awareness at the same time, so people could understand the situation on the ground, what was needed and what the various NGOs were doing. To make it appealing, we came up with combining it with an entertainment programme. Alyque must have been in his forties and was a big showbiz man back then. We took the idea to him, and he very willingly agreed to help us to conduct this event. It was held in the central quad at St Xavier's College, Mumbai. Nothing like that had been done in India before. There was music of all kinds in the central quad—Indian classical, folk, English, dance, poetry. And the inside hall had kiosks of various NGOs which were working in the drought programmes. Food and drinks were in the section next to it. All full of students going from one venue to the other.

Alyque was there throughout, working with us all the time, including the day of the event. He was even the compere for the entire show—it was marvellous because he could bring everything into context. There are very few people who would have that vision and also that degree of skill, theatre, music as well as innovation and creativity, and the desire to really help organizations. He didn't lose sight of helping and freely gave of his time.

Alyque had a tremendous capacity to work with you and bring out the potential of an idea, to help you make it something that was workable. That took vision. And he wasn't interested in doing it for his own name or fame. His joy came from helping people to bring in creativity of this kind. He was also very interested in helping out in social causes.

Conclusion

Your position and status are *not* down to good karma or good fortune. They are a total accident of birth. Are you going to make sure that people who didn't have good luck get some?

I've tried to give 10 per cent of my profits to various charities. I've concentrated on the underprivileged girl child because there we see the great 'accident' of birth. If you are a girl and born in the poorer communities (or the very rich, if you look at the sex ratios in South Delhi) then, oh no! If you're a boy, then the whole world would be open to you.

I mention in my previous book *A Double Life* that when we were celebrating our fiftieth year of Lintas in India, we had a big celebration. That was when I said I wanted to donate money to a campaign that was going to be called the 'Second Freedom Movement: Women need to be free'.

We did it, but the media didn't pick it up. If the media doesn't take it up, it becomes a smaller thing. Could we launch something that could keep the views of women at the forefront? Like a newspaper that always had two views, looking at things that happen from both a corporate and a societal perspective on what the impact of that article had on women?

Incidentally, I don't think it's any coincidence that most of the organizations I mentioned in this chapter (at least Akanksha, Teach for India and Common Purpose) were started by women. Women just seem to have a more compassionate side to them. They are the ones who understand what being a bonus baby is and how it is their responsibility to give back, over and above making money. Perhaps it's because they give birth, I don't know.

BUT: My last wish.

It is time to make 'bonus babies' and giving back to society a social movement, like Gandhi did. Let us not tax the poor even more by not giving them what they need. Vandana often says 'Each one reach one': If every bonus baby supported one person who was not a bonus baby, we could end poverty in months. It does not have to be with money—you can give your time as well. *Think of the hours you spend watching TV or on your mobile phone. What if you did something for the underprivileged instead. The big thing they need is your ear and your time. With that support, the world would thrive.*

We know what we are but know not what we may be.

—*Hamlet*, Act IV, Scene V

Extracting the Essence

- If you are reading this book then, no matter what, you are privileged.
- We use the licence to swindle to justify our position.
- When will we repay the silver spoon?
- Giving bonuses to others leads to a great bonus to ourselves: satisfaction and upliftment.

Hijacking Your Mind—Points for You to Ponder

- What do you take for granted constantly?
- Who do you consistently support, without wanting anything in return?
- How can you be a modern-day unifier?

9

Why Are Terrorists Breaking the Law of Their Very Own Holy Book?

Religious terrorism has horrified the world.

Most of the religions of the world consider it a sin to commit murder. Yet many have so-called believers who have all killed purportedly in the name of religion.

Due to the high-profile nature of some of their attacks, 'Muslim' terrorists and Islam happen to stick out. It has to be said that many other religions have believers carrying out attacks in their God's name, but they don't seem to get the same press. It is also worth mentioning that 'Islamic terrorism' has horrified many millions of Muslims too. But we don't seem to find a way to tackle them effectively. We cannot fight terrorists with guns!

At the root of it, I don't believe that normal, sane, people would join extremist camps. Something must have gone very wrong for them in life if they were willing to take innocent lives as well as their own. Something caused them to become radical, so surely there must be some specific actions that could contribute to de-radicalizing them as well?

I wanted to look at ways to disarm the terrorists without having to physically fight them! There are of course many, many ways to do this. But the AP way?

> *ALYQUEISM: Let's reposition terrorists to show them for what they truly are: hypocrites.*

Ridiculous Ideas Are Where the Future Lies

In 2008, I got this absolutely ridiculous idea. I was reading about Salman Rushdie, and then on the same page I saw that terrorists had struck somewhere or the other in the world. And I said, 'I'm sure in the Quran there must be something against killing innocent people.' I did some research and it appeared that others had had the same idea. But no one had taken it up on a war-footing (no excuse for the pun) and done it on a national and international level of any seriousness at that time.

After talking to a few people about this, a friend of mine got some maulanas (Islamic experts) to come to my house. I said to them, 'Is it true that the Quran says you can kill innocent people?'

All three of them looked very shocked and said, 'Sir, *kya bolte hai aap?* (Sir, what are you saying?) In the Quran it is written that if you kill a single innocent person it is like killing the whole of humanity. And suicide too, is not acceptable in our religion.'[1]

I said, '*Accha*, then why aren't you preaching this?'

They said, 'Yes, we are . . . we are preaching it.'

I said, 'Where?'

'In the masjid.'

I said, 'But those are people who know the Quran. What about all the other non-Muslims who don't know that this is written in the Quran? In that case, how do you not condemn the terrorists, because they are killing innocent people, killing people in buses or in airplanes or railway stations or bazaars, all innocent people who have not done them any harm? And yet they blow them up? Now you need to take it out of the masjids and see if we can spread this message across the world.'

They said, 'Sir, *Hum log to communications expert nahi hai. Aap hai, to aap sochiye.* (We are not the communications experts. You are; so you tell us.) Yes, we would like to publicize this, that those people who are doing that are not Islamic.'

I said, 'I have thought about it. And what I suggest is that you talk to the Grand Mufti who is the head of the Darul Uloom Deoband, where the Sunni movement began. Ask him why he doesn't send out a fatwa against those who kill innocent people?'

They agreed.

Two months later they came back to me and they said that the Grand Mufti had agreed.

I said, 'Yes, but what is the occasion?' They said, 'There's going to be a huge meeting in the Ram Lila grounds' (where Anna Hazare and Baba Ramdev protested against corruption in 2011[2]).

'We are having a meeting there of at least 1,00,000 Muslims, and the Grand Mufti is going to read out the fatwa.' They asked me to draw up the English version.

So I drew up a proposal. I wrote that it is written in the Quran that if any Muslim kills a single innocent person, it's like killing the whole of humanity. And anyone who does that, therefore, has broken the law of the Quran and cannot be considered Islamic. In other words, *excommunicate the terrorists.*

The False Narrative

We have to ask ourselves, why are we calling them Islamic? IT IS WRONG, totally and completely wrong. It has no validity in Islam, because what they are doing is killing people. It's not Islamic, so they're using Islam as a false narrative. Why don't we call them 'Nakli Islamists', *nakli* meaning the people who are going against the law of the Quran?

On 30 May 2008, at the Ram Lila grounds,[3] the Grand Mufti read out the fatwa. He said unequivocally that any Muslim who kills an innocent person is breaking the word of the Quran, which means they are no longer a Muslim.

I was so thrilled, you know, but I unfortunately made one mistake: I left the publicity in the hands of these guys. They had said, 'We will handle it in all the media.'

But they didn't, and consequently the next day there was one column, about six inches, buried near the back somewhere, with the headline saying, 'Deoband first: A fatwa against terror'. That's all. Very few television people came. None of the other press came and I was very disappointed. This was one of the biggest ideas I'd ever explored, and it was a very important idea.

And so I really wept tears of blood you might say, and I then spoke to them again. 'Are you going to do anything further?' They said, 'Yes, we are. We're doing another one, but this time we will really organize the media.' However, subsequently they got busy with other things.

As I said, others have also talked and written extensively about this idea. Islamic scholar Dr Muhammad Tahir-ul-Qadri wrote a 500-page document on terrorism and suicide bombings. I attended his lecture in Mumbai back in 2012, where I was quoted in the press as saying that Islamic terrorism is an oxymoron in the English language and that true Muslims will never practise terrorism. I remain emphatic that terrorists cannot call themselves Muslims.[4]

Is it possible to use this idea again with other strategies to kill the desire to become or stay an extremist? Could the fatwa be reinvigorated on a global platform, with the support of governments, religious leaders from different global Islamic communities and NGOs that work in this field? An idea will peter out if there is no people power behind it. What we need is to galvanize the might of many. Many who join believe, because of what they have been told, that they are superior and that their religious beliefs are superior. With consistent collective messaging, the message will start to take hold in the minds of those who have been brainwashed into believing the nonsense of terrorism and its black-and-white thinking. It does not create belonging (a factor that many say encourages the youth into extremism) and was certainly not decreed by God.

We have over a billion people in India—that's approximately 18 per cent of the global population, plus goodness knows how many more outside of India. Can we unite, to get this issue to stay in the forefront of the mind of our global leaders? It will benefit our country greatly, as well as the rest of the world. It will also certainly remind moderate Muslims of their duties as true Muslims. And it might also start limiting the support that others provide to these Nakli Islamists.

De-sympathize the Supporters

It is not just the terrorists, but the supporters of those terrorists who need to be dealt with. I worked with Chandrababu Naidu from 2001 to 2003 as his communications advisor.[5] I was asked to meet the police commissioner as they had a Naxalite problem—as you know, it is quite severe in Andhra Pradesh. One of the key discussions we had was that the only reasons that the Naxalites or any terrorists exist is that they have a network of sympathizers. Not supporters, but sympathizers. So they have safe houses where they can hide. Remember, there are probably only 10,000 Naxalites in the whole of Andhra, which has got fifty million people, yet the police could not get to them, because they have sympathizers.

Another aim of the fatwa would be to powerfully accelerate some collective action in the Muslim communities, so sympathizers would suddenly begin to realize that there's no point. If there were action groups empowered to spread such messages, especially in sympathetic communities, then true Muslims would say, 'These terrorists are not even Islamic, why should we help them?' Those who kill innocents are hereby excommunicated. This would help reduce recruitment into these organizations. Young would-be suicide bombers would be daunted to break the laws of the Quran. Every young would-be suicide bomber who thinks that's the stairway to heaven would suddenly realize that it's against the Quran, therefore it's not the path to heaven at all. In fact, it leads straight to another place.

Look, I know this is a touchy, thorny issue, and it is much more complicated than I am making it out to be. I know many people do realize it is non-Islamic but still justify their approach through different interpretations of the Quran. I do know there is also diversity in the Muslim communities. What I am saying is we can't just sit back and allow the extremism to continue and cause damage to the millions of innocent Muslims who have no part in it. A global fatwa, backed up with *consistent work of religious groups, NGOs and governments*, can reduce both the number of extreme terrorists and the sympathizers who incorrectly support them. It should also put pressure on Islamic countries to declare their agreement with this and stop tacitly supporting the groups hiding in their countries. We cannot give up on this issue until the next 9/11 or 26/11 happens. We need to deal with this NOW.

If we are not afraid to fight this, with Muslims and any other religious extremists, then gradually, perhaps in the time of your great-grandchildren, the nomenclature 'religious terrorism' will be neutralized.

So I'm saying it's possible and that true Muslims do believe that terrorism is a sin: killing people doesn't solve anything.

Maybe that will come. Let me tell you one good thing that has come out of understanding the scriptures and this same point. Nine terrorists were shot dead during the 26/11 Mumbai attacks in 2008. CNN quoted the Indian Muslim Council as saying that they 'did not want the terrorists buried in Muslim cemeteries because they have defamed the religion'.[6] So somehow the message is creeping in. But now with modern means of communication, it would be wonderful if this message could sweep across the world, in headlines, and not be buried on some page somewhere, because that's what we want. We want people to be more deeply aware that it is anti-Islamic to kill an innocent person.

It is not just about Islam though. Whilst I am all for a united India, we cannot have Bhakts or fanatics from other religions allowed to terrorize either. That includes upper-caste Hindus and conservative Christians. These groups do as much destruction of the mind and body as Islamic terrorists, but they are not called out enough. And in some ways, they are all breaking the tenets of what their religion ultimately stands for. All these terrorists need to be held to account.

We need to reposition religious terrorists across the world to show them for what they truly are: non-believers.

> Had I but served my God with half the zeal I served my king,
> he would not in mine age have left me naked to mine enemies.
>   —*Henry VIII*, Act III, Scene II

Extracting the Essence

» Religious terrorism is a major cause of distrust in the world, especially for innocent Muslims whose reputation is tarred by their nakli siblings.
» Religious terrorists are cowards who go against their holy books.
» If their sympathizers disown them, religious terrorists have limited support.
» A global, concerted effort based on the authentic teachings of most religions can help reduce extremism.

Hijacking Your Mind—Points for You to Ponder

» Where do you not play your part in societal conflicts?
» What have you done to play your part in making a safer world for our great-grandchildren?

10

I Speak to God Every Night. Pity You Can't

Creation's God

Everyone who knows me will say one thing about me for sure: I'm a very open-minded person. Take my views on religion and my relationship with God. This chapter is going to show you that you should consider getting rid of the claptrap in your life and be a bit more open-minded about everyone's religion. You will see why shortly.

A while ago, someone I know (quite devoutly religious) came to me, shaking his head, and said, 'Alyque, you don't believe in God?'

I said, 'I do I believe in a creator, but I don't believe in *your concept* of God.'

When you look around with an open mind, you can't help but realize that God is really in everything around us. I mean, take for example the intricacies of nature. Just look at how beautifully designed nature is, from flora to fauna to even fungi! I couldn't possibly say, 'Oh, this happened by accident.' The whole idea of photosynthesis is mind-boggling. What about the fact that our planet circles this gigantic ball of fire and just happens to be at the right temperature with all the right ingredients to bake life into everything? Genius! And almost impossible to fathom all this creation could have happened without a supreme force somewhere.

Now religion on the other hand, for me, is not genius. It is simply the word of people who lived a long time ago. Quite honestly, we have no hope of knowing whether events happened in the way they are written in the literature available today. I certainly don't believe in organized religion, because as soon as you organize religion, what happens? Humans set up hierarchical systems of self-purported 'emissaries', whichever religion you take, whether Hinduism, Islam or Christianity. And that's what I don't believe in. It ends up becoming such a conventional way of approaching God.

So, I believe in a creator and every night I pray, but to an amorphous God. I don't know what the hell on earth 'He' or 'She' looks like. I just talk to God about things I think are important, like peace in the world.

The Creation of Religion

Religion did not grow from a tree, as nature did. Religion, like advertising, was invented by humans for a purpose. I personally think religion came into the world for two reasons.

One reason was that humans were always fearful, and they yearned for, nay, *needed* a giant protector. For example, 'God will save me from this tiger that's about to eat me up,' or 'God will give me more children, because my children died of some disease.' It didn't always have to be positive. The giant protector was also allowed to rough up humans. If there's an earthquake, 'See, God is angry with me, so he destroyed my house, or possessions or whatever.'

And the second reason for inventing our gods is to have words laid down as guiding principles for living. All religions have some sort of holy book, whether it's the Sikhs who have their Guru

Granth Saheb, Christians with their Bible, Muslims with their Quran, Hindus with their Bhagavad Gita or the Parsis with their Avesta. They all have some form of codification on how to be a good person, mostly through their stories.

So really, religion started as a way of protecting society and enforcing certain codes of conduct. The Ten Commandments is definitely one of the most renowned codes of conduct. And remember, it was invented at a time when we didn't have a well-designed police force, constitution or law court. Religion, in a sense, created a moral order and kept law and order under control. Once law and order were established as separate from religion, then the great need for religion should have dropped away.

It didn't.

It became the overarching moral policeman.

Religion became a kind of police force with a moral right to condemn people. With 'Forgive me father for I have sinned' and such things, religion went much further than the police ever could. It somehow entered our homes and hearts in a frightening way.

But I've always believed that God is within us in a positive way. In other words, instead of being worried about what God would think, we should just try to behave in a godly way—a way that would make Her/Him proud. At the end of this book, I've put down my interpretation of what a godly way could be: a suggestion for the way that society could behave, without having too many rules and regulations. Have you ever thought about putting down on paper your thoughts about your own code of conduct ? You might be surprised with what you come away with.

*ALYQUEISM: Why should we have an emissary for the Almighty?
It's like having a brand ambassador—here, go talk to God on
my behalf.
Talk to God yourself, if God is with you. I talk to God every day.*

Questioning the Unquestionable

I'm sorry, but I am about to be outrageous again. Nature has seasons, and one of the side effects of the seasons is healthy growth over time, because each season's purpose in nature is different. In winter, all that is unnecessary is stripped down. In spring, everything starts to grow. In summer we see full bloom. And in autumn, we start getting ready for winter by paring down. Change is the only constant, and nature consistently sheds what she doesn't need.

Even within the law, we have a system for going back to laws that were created years ago and updating them, like overturning the law that criminalized homosexuality.

Hopefully, you can see where this is going.

If change is a constant and everything is renewed, when, oh when, are we going to update our religious books?

Surely some parts of religion should be done away with, like all unnecessary laws and codes that have outlived their usefulness? And because we don't update religion, because it is sacrosanct as it is purported to come out of the mouth of God or human prophets, we cannot touch it! So we are left with old, outdated ideas such as that, for example, praying at home is a good thing but praying in a church or in a mosque is the real way to pray and God will listen.

Wouldn't it make sense to update some of the ludicrous ideas in religion, or at least admit that times have changed? For example, do you know the Bible says, 'Does not the very nature of things teach you that if a man has long hair, it is a disgrace to him?'[1] So all heavy metal singers and some footballers are a disgrace in God's eyes?

The Torah states, 'And a man who lies with a woman who has a flow, and he uncovers her nakedness, he has bared her fountain, and she has uncovered the fountain of her blood. Both of them shall be cut off from the midst of their people.'[2] Uhm, I think that would mean half the current population of the world should be exiled!

In Islam, there is a passage narrated by Abu Huraira who reported Allah's messenger as saying: 'None of you should drink while standing; and if anyone forgets, he must vomit.'[3] OK so that's most of humanity that needs to vomit, probably quite a few times a day.

Isn't it time to challenge these old doctrines that don't serve us? They just sit around in our lives like an appendix—it's there in the body but has absolutely no use in most adult human beings.

The question is, why haven't these doctrines been challenged if they don't serve us? Why are they still around?

It is not a coincidence.

It is because they still serve somebody.

The Self-Serving Hand of God

The various religions were the first and are probably still the largest global 'organizations'. They have done an incredible job of marketing and selling, and opening offices or outposts in all corners of the world, to encourage others to jump on their (not so) merry bandwagons. And this is only possible because like all good companies, there is a hierarchy of people doing specific jobs. But like all bad companies, what the boss says is the final word.

In the past, the Pope was like the King of the Catholics. He (not she of course) was pretty much unquestioned in his decision-making. Below him, he had bishops, then priests and then the parish priest and all these people were ordained with powers of the religion. For example, the power to marry people. It was the same with all other religions, although the designations and names changed. Only 'priest' level people could marry people, so he became a kind of a Mini God and Mini King. Like this, all sorts of edicts came in that gave them rights and you, as the minion, had to follow their 'wisdom'.

Eventually, you found that unless you attended a mass or a religious meeting you couldn't talk to God. The Catholic Church then took it a step further, where they then told you that you must say a Hail Mary as a punishment for having evil thoughts. Confession was another example where it was only a priest who was able to give you a penalty. Before we knew it, in all major religions, you had to be in the presence of self-appointed masters to get your appointment with the greater power.

Religion needs to move on. How on earth can we evolve as human beings if we are chained to religions that want to stand still?

I was talking to a priest the other day, and I said, 'You know, Father John, you are no longer necessary.'

He said, 'What do you mean?'

I said, 'Why do we need ambassadors to God? Why can't we speak to God directly? Every night I speak to God.'

He said, 'Does God answer your prayers?'

I said, 'No, I don't expect him to. I don't even know if there is a God, but why do I need a priest to be in between as the in-between? We don't need intermediaries.'

He was not happy with me! I continued, as I usually do, 'Father John, on top of this, religion gives us a whole set of rules. Don't do this, don't do that. I went to college. It was a good college. It taught me how to think clearly. Why do I need ambassadors to speak to God and rules that have been created by people I've never even heard of?'

He mumbled something and looked away.

It was not enough for me, so I said, 'And why do you insist that people come to church on Sundays and ring the bell?'

Now he chuckled and finally had an answer, 'To drive away the devils.'

All this is claptrap! Ask yourself what is this claptrap bringing to your life?

For me, it comes back to the fact that we have been brainwashed into accepting religion and all its claptrap because our elders told us to. When I hear 'the elders', I grit my teeth, as so many of the elders are really just dumb cops who want to toe the religious party line, without any questioning.

Personally, I think that priests and their equivalents are like ingrown toenails: toenails serve their usefulness as they cover the toe, but once they are ingrown they cause damage to the human body. I think the time has come for us to abolish priesthoods of all kind.

Another reason to abolish them is that very often they've already become very corrupted. I don't mean money-wise. I mean by abusing their power, which they say is God-given. Look at the cases of sexual abuse that are coming up in the media, from the Catholic scandal[4] to India's Ram Rahim Singh.[5] This has caused many people great misery, all in the fake name of religion. Even the Old Testament's Ten Commandments talk about a world that is long forgotten, but staunch Christians blindly go on following the Ten Commandments, causing even more unhappiness. I bet those same Christians order off Amazon on a Sunday—does that respect the Sabbath?

So, if you truly believe in God, you should be able to talk to God anytime, anywhere without an in-between.

I am therefore against all forms of rules and regulations that don't seem to have an advantage to the individual who has to live under them. A priest does not necessarily have the ear of God. We are led to believe that, but it's not true. We have to re-examine such rules and regulations, otherwise we are constantly living in the past and the only thing that seems to live in the future is technology.

So clearly, you can see that I think human society and its rules and regulations have got to be hijacked and rethought!

In Any Case, Why Are You Your Religion?

I was speaking at a conference for university students. I asked a young man, 'What religion are you?'

He replied, 'Hindu.'

I asked, 'Why a Hindu?'

He looked at me, shocked, and said, 'Well, I was born a Hindu.'

I asked him, 'Why were you born a Hindu? In the womb were you a Hindu?'

His eyes were incredulous, 'No sir. My father was a Hindu, so when I was born, I was a Hindu.'

I persisted, 'So, you have never questioned that?' He said, 'No sir.'

And that's the problem—people just don't question. It's amazing. Even in college, when they should be questioning everything.

Look, I am NOT saying that you should NOT follow your parents' religion. I am just saying that it should not be mandatory, the way it is at the moment. In this day and age, doesn't it make more sense to learn about all religions and then when you are older, choose which one resonates with you (if any)?

Conclusion

> The devil can cite Scripture for his purpose.
>   —*The Merchant of Venice*, Act I, Scene III

Question everything, especially about religion and what is poured into our minds and forced down our throats. Why do we say the 'Father, the Son, the Holy Ghost'—why not 'Mother, child, Holy Ghost'? So, swerve into the future and go off the road to evolve. Stop following silly rules made up by people who lived thousands of years ago and start thinking for yourself.

The word 'society' is, I think, a misnomer. It means people will all think alike and act alike. It is not true: we are all individuals. Religions have been one way of stamping out individuality. Religion is like a routine. You do things because it is laid down very clearly. You go to church on Sundays, you always give to charity. And if you want to be a good Christian or a good Muslim or whatever, certain rules are made for you to understand and to follow. Like all Christians say prayers at bedtime, or all Muslims must pray five times a day. It ends up confining people and stripping away their uniqueness by getting them to live in fear of their individuality. Religion promotes a kind of herd mentality, where we are all like sheep brought in to herd, where everyone should look the same and think the same and should be governed by rules—if anyone breaks them, they are sent to religious jail. All in the name of a God that none of these 'holy' men have ever met, all who say that they know what it means to be godly.

Don't you realize that there is no one on earth who has all the qualities of God? Why not, instead, find bits of God in everyone? Find a lot of people who have got different qualities that you admire and start living by the principles that are important to you.

Postscript

Secularism is letting people choose their own religion and religion is about being told what to do. We don't need a Jesus Christ or Lord Shiva to tell us what to do. Of course we need a home, food on the table, a job, but after all that, are you happy? And if you're not, think why are you not happy? Are you happy when you are helping people? Are you happy when you are acquiring knowledge? None of these things may necessarily make you richer, but they will no doubt enrich you. And if that is the case, how much religion is then necessary?

God and Alyque Padamsee

Cyrus Broacha

TV Anchor, Theatre Personality, Comedian, Author, Podcaster

First, let me at the outset clarify I had a very interesting relationship with Alyque. We met on several occasions, and our opening lines were always exactly the same. My line was, 'Hi Alyque.' His was, 'Who are you?' Actually I'm being a tad uncharitable. Later on his reply would evolve to, 'Not now', 'Please shut up', 'Close the door on your way out'.

When his daughter Raell or, as I knew her then, Rael, asked me to pen a few words, I initially suggested doing what most of us Indians do. That is, asked her to pen them herself, and then have me sign the piece. However, much worse sense prevailed, which means I have to actually read the whole goddam thing, and then seriously pen a few words myself. And with two years of a pandemic, I ran out of excuses. Plus Raell, sorry Rael, is stronger than me.

OK, now let's move on to some little-known facts about Alyque. Facts which my research team dug up after painstaking research. And by team, I mean just me. And by painstaking research I mean, I asked Raell, who used to be Rael.

Here goes. Alyque was tall. His first name wasn't actually Alyque. Also, Alyque was tall. He was either that last of the absolute liberals or the first and possibly only one. And by 'liberal', it doesn't mean he was left leaning. Definitely a free thinker, as rare to find as a Parsee is these days. Also, he was tall.

The chapter on God is an interesting one. He doesn't deny the existence of God, but prefers using the phrase 'Creator'. With a rider, the possibility of the existence of the creator. That's the key one for me. That, and that he was so tall. The fact that he questioned. Isn't that the path to free thinking, democratic thought, I dare say even egalitarianism?

By questioning? It's a bit of a paradox, that 'nothing' is sacred in a sense means respect for all. This, for me, was the essence of Alyque. And of course, that little-known fact that he was tall. So, without confirming or denying God, he makes the only acceptable point for me. That defining answer I got, many a time and oft, in my youth, upon asking a lady on a date . . . 'Maybe.' Clearly ahead of his time. Clearly free thinking. Clearly daring to dream. And even if the last one sounds like a view from a Ms India contestant, it's still largely a noble pursuit.

How's this for a touch of irony? The man known as 'God' in theatre and advertising isn't too sure about the concept and prefers the phrase 'Creator'. And, now when you think of it, he was actually more 'Creator' than God. On stage, in print and television, even as a TV panellist. TV panellist, sadly, is the last bastion of the creative community. By the way.

'Tughlaq' was a visionary. Othello misunderstood. Evita rose out of nowhere like the phoenix. Alyque was parts of all the above. Plus, he was so tall.

In the words of his favourite, 'Here was a Caesar, when come such another.' A free thinking, creative, righteous Caesar. Plus, you can tell from his writings, he was very tall. Very tall.

Extracting the Essence

- Alternative concepts of God need to be acknowledged.
- Religion is used far too often as a moral policeman in control of our happiness.
- You do not need an intermediary to talk to your Creator.
- No one on earth has all the qualities of God consistently demonstrated, so relax!

Hijacking Your Mind—Points for You to Ponder

- Have you really read the religious doctrines you profess to believe in?
- What parts of religion do you think need updating? Whom have you talked to about it and if not, when will you?
- Who is suffering in the name of religion? And what can you do about it?

PART II

RESTART!

11

Speaking the Unspoken Dialogues

Taboos—Breaking the Handcuffs

By now, you have got the hang of this book. I hope each chapter is titillating you and tickling your fancy and you are taking away some nuggets of wisdom to add to your own armoury of thoughts. But there is more to come. In this chapter, I want to examine what we *don't* speak about and honestly question WHY. I want to encourage you to consider having these conversations to bring you greater freedom in your life. Freedom to think. Freedom to consider. Freedom to choose your view. Freedom to publicly express it, whatever it is, so others feel the freedom to discuss it too.

The Protocol Prisons

I coined the term 'Protocol Prisons' many years ago, as I saw too many people trapped and unhappy because of them. These prisons don't actually exist in the real world, unlike nature and the stars in the sky. Yet anyone would think they are more real than the physical world we live in.

But what are 'Protocol Prisons'?

Protocol prisons are conventional attitudes. Whenever we come across a conventional attitude that does not necessarily fit with the times and we STILL choose to follow it, we have effectively been imprisoned by our upbringing. Whether it's religion that says don't eat beef, to a point where we're willing to kill other people for just carrying beef—all these rules and regulations that govern our life are in fact keeping us in mental chains. And you know that all the ideas in this book are meant to hijack your mind, to release you from those protocol prisons that you are forcing yourselves to live in.

This chapter runs through some of the greatest taboos that we have that are not talked about and debated enough. I am not saying my view is right. I am just saying, unlock the mental doors to your protocol prisons and *examine why you think what you think.* Talk to your friends and family. Check if the logic stacks up today, or whether these are ghosts of yesterday that you subconsciously insist on being haunted by.

> *ALYQUEISM: Why do you want to live your life in protocol prisons?*
> *If your mind defines, you will be confined.*
> *So, break those bloody self-imposed handcuffs!*

Taboo 1: Thou Shalt Deny the Caste System Exists

I know I am likely to ignite fury, but from my perspective, India is doomed by the caste system. We are told from an early age that people should know their position and status in society. Yet the tide is turning. Many millennials are saying, 'To hell with that. We will go abroad if we can't be considered equals here!' Although there are problems there too. I have heard of cases as far as Silicon Valley where the issue of caste has reared its ugly head. So really, we need to do something about it, and it starts in India, where we invented the damn thing.

Look, I know that everyone is very conscious of status, and I say fine, there's nothing wrong with that. But what if it is purely based on what you have inherited? I mean, if you are a great Olympic athlete, of course you have a status, but that's *by winning by your own effort*. That is not by your own birth where you are forced to stay within the caste system. You can't move to the next level; you have to stay where you are.

This is something I have always felt passionate about, so I worked with the Dalits on this in Mumbai. I remember when a local Dalit committee, a group of about ten people, came to see me. They greeted me and looked at me with so much reverence that it was shocking for me to see.

They said, 'You're a great convertor of people by changing their thinking from one way to another way. Can you do something about our cause?'

I said, 'Look, I feel for you, but I will never know the true extent of what you go through. So for me, the first thing I want to do is *not* do the talking. I want each of the ten of you to tell me what it's like to be a Dalit. I may have read about it, but I don't know about it first-hand.'

And each one told me the most terrible stories. One man said, 'I am a Dalit and we had to live outside the village, away from others, because of my caste.' Can you imagine that kind of exclusion? What would that do to your self-esteem?

It turns out that there was a little patch of land outside a village where the Dalits were forced to live. They even had to ask permission to come into the village. They were not allowed to drink from the village well, so they had to make their own arrangements to get water. But then they ran out of water. They asked the village for support, but it was met with resistance. Finally, when they were at death's door, the villagers said, 'OK, but you must bring your own bucket. You are forbidden from using our buckets. You can draw the water, but please see that everything that you bring there is taken away. We don't want any trace of your objects or presence to remain.'

The villagers were literally treating the Dalits like they had a contagious disease.

But remember, a contagion can be cured. Being a Dalit cannot.

These villagers were being anti-Dalit in all ways and were intent on making sure the Dalits knew 'their place'.

To cure these villagers, we have to cure the mind. Actually, it's not the mind, it's the protocol prison the villagers are living in. How do we show the villagers that it is not right to do this? How will affirmative action for Dalits ever cure this disease of the mind?

The problem lies with the mindset and millennia of entrenched customs from the Brahminical perspective.[1] Over the years, the Brahmin community's relationship with God afforded many doors to be open to them, and therefore also gave them access to the best education. They hold the invisible laws of permissible interaction in their hands.[2] The Brahmin community is actually one of the largest forces in the country.[3] Others watch them and copy. The Brahminical perspective ensured caste networks play a role in every sphere of your life, at every age—they give you a sense of belonging, get you jobs, identify marriage partners and run your social life. They are so tightly knit in certain fields that it's difficult for outsiders to get in. Over time, higher-caste communities have held on to the power and the opportunities to keep themselves up and the Dalits down, as evidenced by all the horror stories that have been reported. So how can the Dalits fight that, even if the Dalits' thinking has changed?

But it is not just the higher-caste communities any more. I argue it's *all* of us, in one shape or the other. We have no dignity of labour in India whatsoever, and we are responsible for it. Think about how you treat the security guard, your domestic help, or the local *kirana* guy? Do you make time to interact with them? And if you don't, surely you can see you've created your own version of the caste system—those whom you will talk with, and those who are no different to the air you breathe: invisible. Your version of the caste system could be stopping the next Leena Nair or Abdul Kalam from being discovered. Think of how many wasted lives there are in the Dalit community. And what they go through every day.

My heart still bleeds. And we need to talk about this. Because only by talking about this can we address it. Remember, for years, it was illegal to be gay. But then enough people spoke up, and we now have much more acceptance in society; many are allowed to love whom they choose. But why oh why, are we still in this mess with Dalits?

The issue of the eradication of the caste system has been on the national table since Dr B.R. Ambedkar's time. There are national-level political parties as well as advocacy and rights groups for precisely this. When President Obama was elected, many Indians felt a sense of pride. They felt that finally America had accepted racial diversity and by extension made space for them to be included.

But those same Indians forget that pride when they look around their own country. Many north Indians still have this mentality that fair complexion is better and that dark-skinned people should do menial work, which is considered 'dirty' or 'beneath' the higher castes. We have to alter the narrative here. But without a lot more people speaking up about it, how can we *visibly* change the game for our children and the next generations? This is a modern-day atrocity that belongs back in the caveman era. Let's have the conversations with each other, to reaffirm to others that it is not acceptable and that differentiation should never be allowed based on caste. It must be acknowledged across the country—not just in the villages, but across the metros as well. Open your eyes to it and acknowledge the reality of our society; then do something about it.

How can we bring in dignity of labour? What would it take for you to treat your cooks, drivers and plumbers like your friends?

How can we build more equity in India? How can we kick these old systems into the past?

Taboo 2: Thou Shalt Fear Thine Own Death and Speak of It Never

People of late ask me about being close to death. They ask me if I am frightened of death. I say, as Shakespeare did in Julius Caesar:[4]

'Cowards die many times before their deaths;
The valiant never taste of death but once.
Of all the wonders that I yet have heard,
It seems to me most strange that men should fear;
Seeing that death, a necessary end,
Will come when it will come.'

Why do we have this morbid fear of death? We say, God forbid if he or she should die, then what happens?'

How stupid! We will all die when our time comes. So why not talk about it openly? Why does it have to be in hushed tones? Do we really think we can bring on death simply by discussing it?

Sometimes I think in India we are still way ahead of the rest of world when it comes to accepting death. At least we give people the opportunity to see the body of the departed person and come to terms with their feelings. We see the body burnt and there is a finality. The person has GONE. Often in the West there is a closed casket, which only close family and friends see. It is all very hidden away, like sweeping a person under the carpet. Yes, they have gone, but let's not deal with seeing them gone. Having said this, in India there is still an embarrassment around discussing death, particularly in practical terms.

Did you know that all over rural India, it has been difficult to sell life insurance policies? Despite it being a damn good thing for the family, because if the father dies, the family would be without income and life insurance would guarantee they got a payout. However, village men don't want to get it, because they believe they are tempting fate and that something will happen to them. Women don't want to get it for the same reason—that people will think they want their husband dead. They are scared of jinxing themselves, because death is just not talked about openly enough. Until we start having open conversations, using the word death and normalizing it, we will have superstition winning every time.

Open conversations about death are essential for us to be more comfortable about life. Although it is very sad when someone passes on, it is equally unbearable to watch someone who is terminally ill and in extreme pain, finding it difficult to live. People who are 'existing', not 'living', yet society and laws dictate that they must suffer and cannot be put out of their misery. They are the walking dead—no, the hobbling dead because they can't walk any more. Every breath they take is like inhaling sand into their lungs. It is so hard to watch people having to live when their physical organs start failing. They want to pass on their terms. With the population of the elderly growing at an increasing rate in the world, there are not enough hospices or professional staff to make their lives more comfortable.

So, while we are at it, let's tackle another taboo: why can't people be allowed to die if they are terminally ill and in extreme pain or finding life impossible to carry on with? Look, I am not encouraging suicide in general. I acknowledge there are many out there who believe that life is not worth living—it might be to do with feeling overwhelmed with life or a mental health challenge. They need a whole lot of empathy, counselling and treatment. I am reserving my conversation for those who are in physical pain which is so debilitating that life no longer has any joy for them and it is not going to get any better.

The conversation around 'the right to die' or euthanasia is still at a nascent stage. There are organizations across the world that are trying to have the conversation.[5] It is controversial, but if we do not discuss it, we will never be able to debate the pros and cons. And I realize there is huge potential for misuse. But I do believe that there can be enough laws and compliances around it, to put in enough checks and balances to ensure it is carried out with due care. People deserve the right to die with dignity, and the world is somewhat waking up to it. But did you know that voluntary euthanasia is currently legal in Belgium, Luxembourg, the Netherlands, Switzerland and the states of Oregon and Washington in the US?[6]

I will make an outrageous statement: I think there will be death parlours for euthanasia in every country within the next fifteen to twenty years.

Why not? Fifty years ago, people would say, 'Gay marriage, don't be silly. How can gays get married?' In my youth, the discussion about LBGTQ was scandalous and nothing less than the way we treat death now. In the same way, people may talk about death parlours, but mark my words, they will come up all around the world. If we want to have the right to life, why can't we have the right to death too?

It should be absolutely legal, if a doctor and your psychiatrist agree that you cannot go on living with a terminal illness, with pain or for some other acceptable reason, you should be able to get a certificate that you can go to the death parlour.

So can we start active discussions on death and stop it from being this thing of fear? If the right checks and balances were put in to ensure it wasn't because greedy family members would profit from your death, then perhaps we could rest more easily. When you accept your own mortality, you can start living a little easier.

Taboo 3: Thou Shalt Have No Addictions, and If Thou Dost, Thou Must Never Utter It

I have had a few friends who were drug addicts for many, many years. Genetics shows that these things are built into the DNA and can be inherited. Several of them traced their problems. Often their fathers and grandfathers were alcoholics.

Some of them were as young as fifteen or sixteen when they started taking drugs, either at school or in music bands. The challenge is that it doesn't matter what the drug is—when you get hooked, it's exceedingly difficult to get off it. The feeling it gives you is of euphoria, and that's the feeling addicts chase. Some of them went repeatedly into rehabilitation homes, but nothing, I mean *nothing* seemed to be able cure them.

Now, several of my friends are OK. They ended up giving up drugs but now rely on booze and cigarettes. Ah yes, those legal drugs. But let's not 'tut-tut' them just yet.

Because we are ALL dependent on our equivalent of drugs.

It is just that the government has decided some should be legal and others outlawed.

What are these dependencies? My dependency, I realized only recently, is work. When I'm not working because of illness, I get depressed. Oh you, who *have* to go to the gym. Isn't exercise a drug of sorts? But Alyque, I hear you say, exercise can't *hurt* you. Really? There have been enough cases of people pushing themselves too far and getting severely injured. Isn't that an addiction?

So don't look down on those who are smoking up something mild or something that is acceptable in half the world.

Because your *dependencies might be much more painful for you and your families.*

Sit down and think about it. And think about why you are addicted to work, to sport, to drinking, to men, women or anything else. Why do we separate them into shameful and non-shameful addictions? Why can't we see our addictions as just part of us being human?

Much of this comes from the little we know about WHY people get and stay addicted. Most of our knowledge from addiction had come from research that was carried out in the early part of the last century,[7] where addiction was not viewed as a medical condition but a 'bad habit'.

Many years later, a Canadian scientist, Bruce K. Alexander,[8] who is a psychologist and professor emeritus from Vancouver, Canada, came along. He had studied addiction. He had read up in detail on the previous research where rats had been put in separate cages, isolated and given two bottles. One was water laced with heroin and the other had just water. And scientists had watched which bottle they drank from. And of course, they mainly drank the heroin and died. And on that basis, the government said, 'Oh my God, this stuff is so bad.' But Dr Alexander said, 'Hold on a minute, if you put anyone on their own in a cage, they'd be pretty upset, so let's repeat that same experiment with lots of rats in an area where rats feel very happy.' So researchers built something called 'Rat Park'. It was an L-shaped enclosure—almost 9 m squared. They put loads of different things for rats to do; for example, obstacles, tins for hiding and rolling wheels. They had male rats, female rats and food. Again, they also put the two water bottles all the way around, one laced with heroin and the other normal water.

Would you believe that in Rat Park, very few of the rats got addicted to the heroin water?[9] Dr Alexander and his team ran several experiments with all kinds of permutations and combinations. Each time they compared the drug consumption of rats in Rat Park with the rats they had placed in solitary confinement (which were in the standard lab cages). According to Dr Alexander's website, 'In virtually every experiment, the rats in solitary confinement consumed more drug solution, by every measure we could devise. And not just a little more. A lot more.'

So, his submission was that it's not heroin that's addictive.

It's loneliness and being a misfit that causes us to become dependent on external stimuli.

This also fits into another theory, that if you have an addictive personality, you will find something else to be addicted to if you stop the drugs—for example, you might go to alcohol. If you stopped the alcohol, you might go to cigarettes. If it's not cigarettes, it might be watching the television all day, *but you will always find something.*

What you're not dealing with is the underlying problem, which is the sense of *helplessness and not belonging.*

That was one thing that I found utterly fascinating. And as for every single person I've met who has got issues with society or is a heavy drug user (I don't mean somebody who just socially does marijuana), they really don't feel like they belong in this world. They feel the way the world is running is not something that's conducive to their minds.

Can we start having honest conversations about our real addictions and stop being judgemental about other people's addictions? Can we have open conversations about what might be missing in our lives that makes us so addicted? We might find that the conversation that we have may be part of the medicine we need to dissolve or decrease the habit.

Taboo 4: Thou Shalt Not Speak of Paying for Sex

OK, this is really not talked about enough. From time immemorial, we have had sex workers, aka 'prostitutes'. It is often called the oldest profession in the world. Yet everyone shuns it. Wives won't talk about it. Men deny going to them. So how does that explain that every major city has a red-light district?

Isn't it about time we legalized it, everywhere?

I think sex work should be legalized across the whole world, because sex workers are being exploited. I'm a great believer that the more something is suppressed, the more you create an underworld for that particular product. Sex work in itself should not be illegal. If a woman bakes bread, she's allowed to sell it. If she uses her hands to give a massage, even that's allowed. So why shouldn't she be allowed to temporarily sell a service through her body?

But she should be allowed to do so without having to have a pimp, i.e., she should have the claim over all the money. Nor should women be trafficked or forced into it by anyone: it should be their choice. Why not? Therefore, I mean we should legalize sex work, as long as the woman is in charge.

Sex work is evil only when women are forced into it. And because it's illegal, they are always frightened of being caught by the law, as they will get into trouble, as much as the pimp.

I read an article that said that sex work is legal in over thirty countries. Some of the women said, 'It's my body. Who are you to tell me what I can and can't do with it? What's wrong with accepting money for having sex with a person, as long as he's not trying to force me, and he pays me money. When I had a boyfriend, he used to give me gifts, and here my customer is giving me money . . . why are people so uptight?'

In Hamburg, Germany, there's a place called the Eros Palace, which I think was renamed Pascha.[10] It was massive—multiple stories and spread out over thousands of metres. The women were beautiful, with some reasonably good looking, and they were often dressed in the most flamboyant kind of clothes like at a carnival. Some dressed like ordinary girls. You would chat first, and then they would agree on a price with you. Then they would say, 'Come with me,' and you walked to the first door, where you saw a very clean, almost antiseptic-looking room with a bath attached, and you made love. The money was paid in advance, and you even got a receipt for it. You know, she *had* to give you a receipt. That receipt had to be sent every month to the tax collector: get this, the Germans tax sex workers to pay for building hospitals, schools etc. Like regular working citizens. It is all above board. Nobody can be arrested for being a sex worker, but someone can be arrested for living off the earnings of a sex worker, like a pimp.

Now imagine the dignity of women all around the world if this was the norm instead of exception? At the moment, women are forced to pay up to half their earnings to a pimp who uses a lot of it to pay the police to turn a blind eye to the trade! Where is the logic in that?

Sex is natural. If men have a desire, why shouldn't they pay for the service they receive to the one who has truly earned it? What right do the pimps have to claim any of the women's earnings as their own?

Can we please have some more open conversations around this, across India and across the world? Why shouldn't women have the right to trade their body if they are getting the rewards for doing so? And be protected in doing so?

Taboo 5: Thou Shalt Sell Your Sons to Get a Slave

Izzat or honour.

Although dowry has been prohibited since 1961 by law,[11] we all know what happens in reality. Even though the government has tried to strengthen the law several times in the 1980s, there is still almost one dowry-related death every hour, according to some sources.[12]

In India, the idea of dowry is one of the most dangerous thought processes ever. I realized I had to get the youth to think differently. I got my opportunity when I was giving a lecture in a college years ago. I asked, 'How many of you young men are going to ask for a dowry?'

Only three people out of about fifty raised their hands.

I then asked those three, 'Why would you ask for a dowry?'

One of them shook his head. 'I won't ask for a dowry. My father will ask for a dowry.'

I said, 'Is your father getting married to the girl?'

He laughed and said, 'No, my father will ask for a dowry, otherwise he won't accept the girl.'

I asked him whether he thought that was right, and after a pause, he squirmed. He finally said, 'No, I don't think it's right.'

I asked further, 'So why don't you tell your father that you don't think it's right?'

He looked down at his toes. 'Because he will fire me.'

I said, 'By all means, take the firing, but don't do something that is against your own sense of values. Just remember, in not so many words, you are the one *really being paid for*, like a motorcycle. You are a motorcycle in a shop. The father of the girl comes in and buys you; is that what you want to be—someone who is being bought?'

'No, sir, I don't want that.'

'Your father-in-law is buying you.'

This boy hadn't thought of it like that. He thought he was getting money, but the money was actually a price on his head. *A dowry is nothing more of than the sale of young men.*

This came to me because of a conversation I overheard at university. When I was in college, often at my table, someone would say, 'This girl's family came and we asked for three lakhs, so I guess I'm worth three lakhs.' Everyone laughed.

Then someone else said, 'What are you talking about? I didn't tell you, but last month only, I signed up for five lakhs.'

They were thinking of it as a badge of honour! They did not realize the actual human being that was being bought was themselves.

I felt so strongly about this that I made this idea into an anti-dowry public service commercial. It shows a cattle market, and the camera can see the first buffalo. Next to him is the buffalo's owner and around the buffalo's neck is a price tag. Next to the buffalo is a boy who also has a price tag around his neck. Then the camera pans over to the next one. And again, there's a buffalo with a price tag and again a young man with a price tag around his neck. You go around in a circle, and they all have a price tag, so the audience starts getting it.

I like to get people involved in the irony, through humour.

Well, the ad caused some issues, especially in rural Maharashtra. It was shown in cinema houses and some people threw stones at the screen, screaming, 'What do you mean, we're selling our men as if they were buffalos? We are men!'

But the message hit home, that you're nothing more than a buffalo for sale.

Whichever way you look at a dowry, it is wrong. How dare anyone ask for money from the one who is going to carry on a family name by having children? And is probably going to be an unpaid maid, cook, cleaner, helper and carer over the next decades, until she drops dead? And even if she doesn't do *any of this*, what right do you have to make her parents pay anything?

I know the conversations about dowry have gone on for a long time. But it is still endemic in so many parts of India. *Can we widen the conversations especially amongst young people to enable them to stand up to each other and their parents to honestly make dowry a relic of the past?*

A Solution to the Taboos: The Unspoken Dialogues

The Unspoken Dialogues came about because I realized that a lot of people wanted to share something that was in their heart, but they were unable to. It might have been because of fear, shame or insecurity and as a result, they would otherwise never be able to get it out of their system. They wanted to share this with someone who cared to listen, but did not want to be judged for it.

And I got this idea from a very well-known psychiatrist in Bombay. We were having dinner one night and I asked him, 'What has been your most interesting case?'

He sat back and thought for a minute. Then he said, 'I was flying from London to New York and I was in business class. It was one of those planes where you could not put a divider up between you and the person next to you. And next to me, there was an African American lady. I don't know why, but I said to her, 'Look, this flight is going to take us six to seven hours and we're going to be together for that time. You don't know me, and I don't know you. I don't want to know your name and I'm sure you don't want to know mine. I'll tell you my profession. I'm a psychiatrist. Is there anything you would like to tell me, that you've never told anyone in your life? Something that you kept as a secret, but has always been nagging you? You have an opportunity to get it off your chest.'

She looked at me and frowned. 'Absolutely not. Why would I tell a stranger?'

I said, 'That's the very reason you should tell me, I am a stranger, and you don't know who I am. You're never going to see me again.'

After about an hour or two, she began to get a bit fidgety. I looked at her and she crumbled. She said, 'OK, I'll take you up on that offer.'

And then she told my psychiatrist friend a very interesting story. She said she was married and she found out her husband was having a long-term affair. She was terribly upset and even thought of committing suicide, but she gritted her teeth and stuck on in the marriage. Yet a thought entered her mind, 'How do I take my revenge?' She decided she would do this by having an affair herself.

So, she had an affair with his best friend. Just out of spite.

And she deliberately let him find out. Her husband came to her, distraught, and said, 'I can't believe you're having an affair with my best friend.'

She said, 'Yes, I am.'

He said, 'I beg you, give it up and I'll give up my relationship with this woman.'

She shook her head. 'No, you can give it up, but I'm not going to give it up.'

The psychiatrist interrupted, intrigued, 'But did you love this man, the best friend?'

She shook her head again, 'Not at all, it's a purely mechanical affair, only done to get my revenge.'

He persisted, 'You were causing your husband so much distress.' She nodded, biting her lip.

The affair apparently went on for several years, and she still refused to give it up. Her husband gave up his affair and told her, 'I really do truly love you . . . my affair was just one of those things.'

She said, 'No, to me, my affair is not just one of those things, and I'm not going to give it up. Either you leave me, or we continue as we are, because I tolerated your affair for all these years. Now it's my turn.'

The psychiatrist asked, 'So did you give it up?'

She said, 'No. It's still going on now. But I'm relieved to admit the truth to someone.'

The psychiatrist recounting the story turned to me and said, 'You know Alyque, people have such extreme ways of dealing with hurt. This person dealt with hurt by having an affair. But she looked so relieved that she could talk to someone who would not judge her. And that ultimately was what was important.'

That led me to think that a lot of people will have a secret that they've never told anyone, but they are desperate to unburden themselves.

Inspired, I decided to get people in different situations to tell me what their unspoken dialogue was. At one sit-down dinner, I sat next to a lady and I said, 'Tell me your unspoken dialogue.'

She said, 'You know, my husband and I have been together, but for most of it with our daughter who is not married. She's now forty years old. Honestly, we have never had a proper marriage because she's always been there. She's the, you know, uninvited guest, and we don't know how to tell her. That's my unspoken dialogue. I need to tell her that.'

I said, 'So what's holding you back?'

'How can I tell my daughter to get out of my house?'

I don't know if she ever told her daughter, but she looked relieved after she told me.

The more people I asked, the more people opened up and told me amazing, sometimes crazy stories. So I got hold of some people in theatre and asked them, 'Could you write a sort of short story based on these unspoken dialogues?' And they put them together into short plays.

One is very vivid in my memory, about a woman from Maharashtra. This woman was just coming out of a long relationship. She had gone to a nightclub and another woman came and stood right up close, next to her.

So, I asked her, 'What happened next?'

She said, 'Well, we were both on our own, so we sat at the bar drinking for a bit. She was in Mumbai on a work assignment for a couple of days, and she was telling me about her high-profile job. Then she ran her finger down my cheek and told me I had really pretty eyes. But I could tell it wasn't just a compliment. It was a bit more.'

'So how did you feel?' I asked her.

'Quite honestly, it was a bit of a buzz and I felt a rush of energy go through me.' The woman was squirming by this time as if she was talking about having done something wrong. She looked down at the floor, and she could not look at me. 'One thing led to another, and I went back to her hotel for a coffee. And I ended up . . . you know . . . staying the night with her. It was amazing. But not something I would do again.'

I asked her why.

She said, 'You know, I think it was just the thrill of doing something that was forbidden. And it was fun.' She winked at me, visibly relaxed from getting this off her chest. 'Actually, maybe I'll do it again someday. If I'm truly honest, it was more fulfilling than being with a man.' What an unspoken dialogue.

Then there's the story of another rather unpleasant guy. He was a cleaner who worked at Sion Hospital Emergency room, taking care of all the major accidents that happened nearby. So, the room was always full of blood and corpses and this guy used the dead bodies in his charge by talking to them about all his misdemeanours. He had a way of getting out his unspoken dialogue; only he was never 'heard' by someone living. One story that was in the play was about this man's niece whom he had a crush on. And he talked to the dead body. The corpse was a woman's. He said, 'I have terrible thoughts and I have to talk to someone about it. I'm in love with my niece and my wife doesn't know. I'm telling you, as you won't tell anyone else.'

It's a macabre story. That's his unspoken dialogue.

We ran these plays for quite some time. Then at the end of the show I said, 'Alright, now it's time for the audience discussion. For those that want to stay and open up, stay, those that want to go, go now.'

Almost 90 per cent of the audience stayed and then they began to talk about their unspoken dialogues. Nobody knew anyone. You had bought your ticket and that's it. And they loved speaking up, knowing that no one would say anything.

All this just shows that *we live these very shallow lives where we've got this outer persona and we've got this inner world as well.*

I think most people don't have only one unspoken story. They have several.

And we need to release! How can we build a community of unspoken dialoguers?

Conclusion

Having read this chapter, I want to ask you something. How much are you caged by conventional attitudes?

If I could really hijack your mind, what unspoken dialogues would I find there?

And why won't you let them see the light of day?

Postscript—Bring Sex out of the Closet and the Boudoir

I've always tried to break the rules. That's another thing I love. This is, I think, a schoolboy kind of attitude that I have.

You realize by now that for me, sex is an important part of life. That's why I did something in typical Alyque style.

In response to the *Vagina Monologues*, I did a play called the *Penis Dialogues*, where the penis is referred to quite openly. It was in an auditorium, and a lot of people were shocked at how you could talk in public about the penis and the vagina and about making love.

'Alyque, these are private matters and should remain in the bedroom,' I hear some of you say.

Well, I say, not at all.

In the 1960s, the concept of open marriage was openly discussed, the Wonderbra was created and see-through tops were all the rage. I was in Geneva of all places, a pretty sedate town, very conservative, yet on the promenade there were young women wearing transparent blouses. The purpose was not to create a sensation.

It was very much, 'When I feel like it, I will display my best assets. Just as I would wear mascara to enhance the beauty of my eyes and just as I would use a fairness cream to enhance the lightness of my skin. Or alternatively, wear a tan cream, as if I've been in the sun at a seaside resort to get a lovely tan that makes me look darker, because that is fashionable and attractive.'

Bringing sexual attractiveness out into the open is quite acceptable. So, I think men and women should have that conversation. I think compliments to any part of the body should not be construed to mean you are a sex object. Instead, it should be about you having attractive features, whether your eyes, your breasts or even your vagina. Why should there be anything wrong in that?

However, the man has crossed the line if he says, 'OK, you asked for it, lady. I am going to bang you.'

Understand where the line must be drawn.

Anyway, as I said, when the *Vagina Monologues* came out, I went to see it. I knew the person running that show and it was running successfully because of the title.

When I chose to do the *Penis Dialogues*, there was an instant uproar.

I was called up by the Maharashtrian censorship board. They said, 'You can't say "penis dialogues"!'

I said, 'You can say *Vagina Monologues*. Why are men worse because they have penises?'

They said, 'No, we can't allow it.'

They even came to the show and accosted us at every show.

We continued.

People would say, 'This *Penis Dialogues* sounds like something I'd like to hear,' but it was unlike the *Vagina Monologues*, which is a very serious study of how the vagina is treated. I didn't mean mine to be any revolutionary thing.

It was the first time I started having audience discussions, where they stayed behind after the show. In one audience discussion, an actress got up and said, 'You can't talk about things that belong in the bedroom.'

I said, 'Why do they belong in the bedroom? It's because of the inability of people like you to accept sex as a part of life.'

She said, 'Sex is for the bedroom.'

I said, 'Life goes round and round. Don't treat sex like you've got a tiger in there and it will eat us all up. Nonsense!'

She said, 'What is your ambition? What is your purpose in doing this?'

I said, 'It's to take sex out of the closet. Forget about homosexuality, I want to bring sex out of the closet!'

Give sorrow words; the grief that does not speak knits up the o-er wrought heart and bids it break.
—*Macbeth*, Act IV, Scene III

Extracting the Essence

» We force ourselves to live in protocol prisons of our own making.
» We need to talk about taboo topics, otherwise they fester with age.
» We should alter the way we think about addiction. We all have addictions. Sometimes we just make them out to be passions. They help us with our emotions and our loneliness.
» We all have unspoken dialogues. Perhaps it is time to have the courage to speak up.

Hijacking Your Mind—Points for You to Ponder

» What are your addictions? Be honest.
» What would you most like to get off your chest if you could speak freely? Why don't you?
» What are your other taboos? Why don't you speak of them?
» How can we help others speak their unspoken dialogues?

Thoughts

Tushar Gandhi

Activist, Author, President of Mahatma Gandhi Foundation

While reading the manuscript of this book, I was struck by two thoughts straight off. What Alyque asks us to do to unshackle and liberate our mind. My first reaction was 'No! Never!' The questions and tasks were intimidating. It's easy to disrobe, strip naked, even in public, but it takes a lot of courage to strip one's mind and lay it bare, even to oneself. It calls for a lot of courage.

While I was reading it, I thought of two things from the legacy I have inherited. Bapu, in writing his autobiography, *The Story of My Experiments with Truth*, has done precisely what Alyque asks the readers to do to unshackle their minds. One of the unique features of Bapu's autobiography is how transparently and honestly he has laid bare his life. On reading it, one is left feeling intimate with the writer, knowing the person absolutely. His autobiography was Bapu unburdening his soul, unshackling his mind.

The other aspect of similarity was the narrative. Every sentence of Alyque's book is a challenge—it screams 'I dare you!'. In 1909, Bapu wrote a book in a similar style, challenging and debunking set notions in the society of that time. What he suggested in it was pretty radical for the times. He took on each of the set societal norms and demolished them; pretty 'anarchist' writing for a person of non-violence. The book was *Hind Swaraj*. It was written like a conversation between the writer and the reader. This is how I reacted to *Let Me Hijack Your Mind*.

My response to Alyque on reading it is, 'Thank you dear Alyque, for offering to hijack my mind. You have reminded me that on some accounts I have already hijacked it but hadn't been aware! Thank you for reminding me of the wings I had forgotten I had. You have made me realize that I can soar into the heavens on their strength, myself. And I can choose where to ride piggyback with you!'

12

My One Thousand Best Friends

A journalist wrote to me a year ago asking me how many people I knew well. Not just acquaintances, but where I knew what made them tick inside.

I called back and told him, 'Probably about . . .' I paused for dramatic effect. Then said loudly, 'Yes, probably about a thousand.'

He was quite incredulous. 'A thousand people, really? Mr Padamsee, I know you have lived a long life, but surely you can't know a thousand people that well? Who are they?'

So I said, 'You think so? OK, I will give you their names. I would start with Hamlet, Othello, Juliet, Romeo, Evita, Portia, Puck, Malvolio . . .'

He burst out laughing, in total disbelief.

The fact is that I *do intimately know a thousand people*. Do you know, I did seventy-seven plays, so in effect I have seventy-seven different families, comprising the characters, the cast and all the supporting staff! The truth is that I know characters from plays frankly better than I knew my own children. I never analysed my children, never once sat down with Q or Raell and said, 'What is your real goal in life?' More recently I have started talking to them about it, but not in my younger days.

Although I talked a lot about theatre in my last book *A Double Life*, I felt it would be good to take a chapter to talk about how theatre altered my perspective of life, and then, coming full circle, how I have used theatre to hijack other people's perspectives on life. In fact, I love to talk about theatre and why theatre is life and life is theatre. Because my life is a perfect example of that. To me, my life has been like a rather long unfolding play, with all the plot twists that come with it. I've always followed my heart. Not only in romantic love, but in the work I do and the nurturing I do. It has always been very theatrical. And my approach has inspired other people to do the same.

Quite simply, at an early age, theatre hijacked my life.

My brother Bobby, whose real name is Sultan, was the culprit for my love of theatre. He was a genius—he started the theatre group of Bombay. He's the man who inspired the whole family to be enchanted with theatre. Bobby was a Renaissance man—he was a playwright, an actor, a director, a sculptor; he was everything rolled into one. He was honestly more famous at that time than I have ever been.

Bobby decided, since he had been to Oxford, that they would do plays in English, particularly Shakespeare. He put me on stage in *The Merchant of Venice* in a scene with the Duke of Morocco, who had two little page boys with black faces with him. Bobby was playing the Prince of Morocco, and my other brother and I were the page boys.

There was, of course, the excitement of the rehearsals before the performance. But the buzz on that final night, with getting changed and putting on the black make-up, culminated in the experience of being up there with everyone looking at us. It was overwhelming, in a positive way.

I knew, from that moment, theatre was my life.

How Theatre Hijacked My Life

There is absolutely no point in having experiences if you don't reflect on what they teach you. I have talked about the importance of curiosity in hijacking your life. Well, I want to be able to explain to you how theatre really piqued my curiosity and showed me new directions. It is important to reflect, as then you'll understand how vital it is to have something you are passionate about in your life (other than your main work), that will teach you a different side to life if you allow it to and give you a wider perspective.

My curiosity about theatre was not about the costumes or the sets; they were part of it, but not the main reason.

It was how theatre made both me and the audience think about things, and ultimately ourselves. Vandana uses this term 'insploration' instead of exploration—it is the idea of gaining deep insight into ourselves through our craft. To sports people, they may get that insight into what they need to alter, by watching other players. You just have to listen to Andre Agassi talk about how he wanted to improve his game and learnt to play differently in order to beat Boris Becker's serve, just by watching his tongue.[1]

In my case, many of my insights came through theatre. That's why the use of upfront discussions to understand the playwright's intention was incredibly important to me and I think the reason for my successful productions. In all my plays, even *Jesus Christ Superstar*, discussions commenced three months before we started a single physical rehearsal. For me, doing a play doesn't mean putting it on stage. It means understanding what the playwright is getting at, contradicting it, if necessary, and tearing it to pieces, only to build it back up again with my take on it. We would look at how the play impacted the world at that time, with its values and sentiments. We would study the characters and their intentions. We would think about the setting. It's not a surface discussion, where you throw light on the play and just skate over it. It's an extremely deep insight where you throw a spotlight on the play, then with surgeon-like precision, dissect it completely, take out of it whatever is needed, put in anything missing and then place it back together. That dedicated time is what creates bonding within the team and the final success with the audience.

In addition, growing up with Bobby's plays showed me an alternative life. I mean that. He indirectly taught me that multiple, alternate realities existed within our current lives. The basis for the whole of my life became *people can actually have multiple lives within this one.* So, for me, my multiple lives were about advertising, theatre as well as social issues and nurturing protégés.

From Theory to Practice

So, the journey to understanding the problem and working out the answers is what excites me. That's why I love theatre. I never know how it's going to look finally on stage. That's probably where my ability to plan and organize comes from: you can't allow anything to go wrong on stage, which therefore gives you skills you can use outside the theatre too. I carried this over into advertising and my other interests, and it served me well.

My theatre work has always been work-in-progress. I approach my plays with a totally open mind. I know the players, I know who the characters are, the dialogue is good and I know it has a certain strength. So I just let it unfold, like the waves, and every so often we have a great tsunami of a production.

But there's one thing that all the plays I have done have in common. The plays I chose always challenged the status quo.

And hijacked the rules.

The Emotions of Judas: AP Style

Tirthankar Poddar aka 2Blue
Singer, Orator, Scribe, Storyteller

I was slapped by a cop twenty years ago when I was in business school. It wasn't just another slap. I couldn't eat, see, and hear anything for a while. The experience had left me so broken and paranoid that for the next several years, I couldn't even look at a man in uniform. I had casually mentioned it to Alyque during one of our rehearsals for *Jesus Christ Superstar*.

On a particular night, I wasn't feeling my character's anger enough. Now you see, Alyque had a very deep understanding of emotionality. He knew how to use memory to generate emotions. So, when he needed his Judas (me) to be broken and paranoid, and I wasn't getting it fully, just before I went on stage he slapped me as hard as he could.

And it never failed to get the job done.

The incessant slapping generated the pain and paranoia I needed for my scenes. And from the reviews I read later, I could tell that people could feel what I felt. So, come to think about it, everything happens for a reason. God bless that cop. And God bless AP for making me feel what I felt.

Breaking the Rules

Theatre enabled me to take risks with the rules. I am driven by boredom with the ordinary and I want to see change and excitement. I do that by exploring the new and unknown and going off the beaten track. I go into fantasy land where there are no rules, which is also why I like Vandana's visionary novels about other worlds. She has broken the rules in creating new planets in her book, like I have done in many of my plays.

Theatre is fantasy—it is an escape, so it is possible to break the rules more easily than with most professions. When I said that I was going to do *Julius Caesar* without the Julius—it was going to be a woman instead—it was a huge risk. Then I did it. People said, 'What rubbish is this?' Everyone thought I was mad. But I had to do it. Vandana asks me why I felt so, and I realized usually it stems from, as Hamlet says, 'There's something rotten in the state of Denmark.'[2] Now in *Hamlet*, the King has killed his brother and married his brother's wife—a total misuse of power—in order to gratify himself. So, when I see things that I feel are not right, I need to find a way of getting other people to see that it's rotten.

Theatre gives me that opportunity.

I adapted the Bard's words to give a satirical view of the world, covering issues such as women's insecurities over their size or beauty. In the end, Sabira Merchant, who is a fantastic actress, was an excellent 'Julia Caesarina'.

Disrupting My Perspective

Sabira Merchant
Corporate Trainer, Actor

I'm quite a tiny person. So, when Alyque suggested Julia Caesarina, I was not sure. I always imagined Caesarina to be a big, strongly build woman. But this is where Alyque turned me upside down. He said that no one had to be big or small physically. It's just the part that is within you that pushes you out and gets you there to the audience. And he said, 'You have that power within you to sway them. And that's why I want you to do it.'

And that was the last play that Alyque was going to do.

The Fourth Creator in Theatre

How I think about theatre is conceptually different from how most other people think about it, and this story illustrates it. I had a visit from a professor who teaches Shakespeare at a university in eastern India and who knew of my love of Shakespeare. One of the things I discussed with him is that everyone says there are three creators in the theatre: one is the playwright, the second is the director who has an interpretation of the playwright's work and the third is the actor who plays the role. Out of the three, the only one who is in direct touch with the audience is the actor.

Well, I'm saying that there's a fourth player, or creator, in theatre. The audience is, of course, a particularly important part of theatre. Without an audience, you wouldn't have theatre, it's as simple as that! And the audience has a right to give their opinion apart from clapping and laughing. Bertolt Brecht of course did a lot of this work through 'Epic Theatre'.

Therefore, every play that's worthwhile should have opportunities for the audience to offer their point of view. When the professor heard this, he said, 'You know, I've read about a tonne of books on theatre and I've never heard that in my life. It's very original and I'm astounded people don't do this more often. The audience is the only reason you have theatre and they're the people who never get a chance to give their opinion.' He was hijacked! It changed the way he thought about theatre forever.

I remember that we performed a play called *Death and the Maiden* in Mumbai. It's a play which was first staged in London and subsequently went to New York. A comment was made about those productions and I have since burned it into my memory. It was about the play in New York not being as moving as the one in London. Even the playwright Ariel Dorfman was quoted to have been disturbed to see people clapping and laughing at the intermission, when the production tackled horrifying subjects.

It made him question whether the director had been true to Dorfman's experiences in Chile and the traumas of the past. He felt that if the play had been performed effectively, during the intermission, no one would have been talking about what they would eat for dinner.[3]

Ever since then, my criterion for choosing a play has been that after you see my play, will it go home with you? It must be something that will be lasting and have an impact on your everyday life. It can't just be something to be laughed at and enjoyed . . . no . . . it should be something that lives with you, and that's the crucial part.

That is exactly the reason why I stopped curtain calls. If you allow the actors back onto the stage for that final bow, it makes the audience realize that the play was not real. However, if you just close the curtains after the final scene, something stays inside the audience.

That's when the audience realizes that theatre is life.

The Theatrical Detective

To put on a play that the audience feels truly reflects life, you have to make it totally believable. That goes back to the start of the chapter for me and getting to know the characters. How do you get to know them?

Curiosity.

It all comes back to curiosity and the curiosity of wanting to know my thousand best friends intimately, to examine them so deeply, that I understand their every thought and every motive. Because if I don't to this, the audience won't feel them in the way I want to portray them. As I understand my characters so well, it helps me understand the public over the years—what makes them tick and how to persuade them.

Theatre taught me how to look beneath the surface. To get inside.

Ultimately, I subconsciously used theatre to investigate human nature. I wanted to understand what makes people do what they do. Whether I was doing *Evita*, investigating what this thirst for power and not money is, or *Legends of Lovers* or *Romeo and Juliet*, investigating theories on love, human nature was at the heart of it.

When I was doing the plays, I was unaware that there was a theme of investigating human nature. However, it is as clear as day if you look at my repertoire. My *Romeo and Juliet* was set in Bombay in the Hindu–Muslim riots. She was a Hindu and he was a Muslim, instead of the Montagues and the Capulets. The whole tension came alive in that Mumbai auditorium, in a far more 'real' way than having irrelevant sixteenth-century themes. The audience could feel the danger of falling in love with someone from the opposite side. Let's be honest, Hindu–Muslim relationships are still very much a challenge outside the big cities (even within the big cities actually), and I wanted that to come through.

In *Legend of Lovers*, the theme is different. I wanted to challenge the way we perceive love during our lives. The hero has a clear idea of the woman he has in mind, who he wants to fall in love with. In the audience discussion we had on the first night (we had a discussion every night), one woman confessed, 'I always had a blueprint of who I would fall in love with. He had to be tall, he had to be handsome (all the clichés), he had to be fair, he had to have a lovely sense of humour and he had to be cherishing, nourishing, he had to love me for who I am . . .'

I said, 'Wonderful! Great idea, but did it come true?'

She said, 'Nonsense! It's a stupid idea! I eventually married a man who is none of the things in my blueprint.'

I said, 'Really, how does he feel about that?'

She said, 'Ask him, he's sitting next to me!'

We all have these concepts and ideals. They don't necessarily hold true, but that's the fascinating thing about human beings.

◉

Conclusion

Now when I look back, I am beginning to see the themes of my plays. One was to do with women and women in power, the second was communal divide and how we have the power to repair it. It is worse than the fault lines in the earth's makeup.

Theatre is so important, because in my life, it has taught me much more than advertising has taught me. It has taught me how to understand people and, through this, how to motivate people.

Theatre has also given me the ability to take risks and try all sorts of ideas. I hope these stories will inspire you to break free of those mental chains and take risks!

All the world's a stage, and the men and women merely players. They have their exits and their entrances, and one man in his time plays many parts.

—As You Like it, Act II, Scene VII

Extracting the Essence

- Every group of people you interact with can become a new family to you.
- Progress comes from breaking the rules.
- Observe the reactions of those around you. Work out what they are taking away with them.
- Being a 'detective' in real life throws up real insights.

Hijacking Your Mind—Points for You to Ponder

- What has hijacked your life in the past?
- Which connections have you ignored? Can you reignite them?
- Which rules are you not breaking and why?

13

Smart Alyque's Tips, Tricks and Tools for a Hijacked Life

This chapter will keep your brain on its toes.

You know, a lot of people will say about another person, 'So-and-so is blind to the fact that . . .' and they will give their opinion on why someone is not looking at a particular situation. We need to remember that none of us are blind.

We are just wearing blindfolds.

All of us, including me and you, are wearing blindfolds in some way or another. And if we are wearing them, we can also take them off.

Isn't it time we stopped running like hamsters in blindfolds on a wheel, trying to catch something or the other? And when we do get it, we carry on running on the wheel to catch something else. You know it and I know it. We just do it automatically, as that is what we have been taught to do our whole lives.

NO MORE.

You need to stop existing and start living a full technicoloured life, not a black-and-white one!

People ask me how I have managed to have such a colourful life and fit in multiple careers. Well, the truth is I've had a joyful life because I don't just accept everything. I want to improve it, I want to change it, I want to shake it up.

This chapter is going to introduce you to some powerful ideas that will get you thinking differently. I encourage you to apply them to your life and see what new colours you can discover and then paint your life.

What is the difference between tips, tricks and tools?

Tips are nuggets of my expert advice that I have picked up over the years.

Tricks are special ingenious techniques that I want to share with you.

Tools are frameworks that have served me well and that you can use to reanalyse yourself and your life.

Tips

Be an AP Yourself—An Agent Provocateur

People tell me that after they visit me, they go away buzzing with ideas. That's exactly what happens to people who see my ads. I get both groups thinking about everyday objects differently, which causes an excitement inside them.

A lot of my advertising was considering the same problem, but in a different way.

Think about Liril soap. When everyone was talking about complexion, perfume and good lather, I just said NO, it's freshness.

When I thought about condoms, I said, 'The whole point about the condom, for me, is making love. But nobody says it, so let's make it about pleasure.'

Even though this way of measuring beauty is no longer acceptable, everyone thought about women when it came to fairness creams. So, in that era, I got them thinking about men.

For the whole of my life, I have been getting people to go upside down with their thinking. But I could never realize *how* I would do it, until Vandana came along. I tell her that she is like an alarm clock—continually waking me up. I have realized more about myself through conversations with her, because she constantly prodding me and asking me why I think this way or that way. I've been forced to reflect with her more than a shrink would make me!

I realized that it doesn't matter what you tell me: I will still ask questions to find a way to look at it from a different angle. And I am relentless. If you say it's black, then I'll immediately say it's white and find a way to prove it. I will not stop until I find another perspective AND be able to persuade you of it. Especially when it comes to areas I really care about, like justice and creating equity. I explain my approach to being able to do this later in the chapter, when I talk about OICA.

So I am encouraging you to look at EVERYTHING in your life from the lens of 'it can be changed for the better', and then go through every way you can think of, from the sublime to the ridiculous, to come up with it. Don't settle for anything but a total change.

If that means researching deeply and provoking people to get them to see alternative views, then by all means, please do it. Especially if it means standing up to ideas that you know are not right. Be an Agent Provocateur. And you'll soon become a change agent.

Be Relentless

To un-trap yourself from life's mental shackles, you will have to get creative. And you need two qualities to be creative: relentlessness and curiosity. I think these are two of the most underrated qualities in the world today.

Relentlessness or persistence has gone out the window because we live in a world where almost everything is now available 'on tap', whether you talk about the news or ordering food. Everything is available, everywhere and at all times. The media even make our entrepreneurs out to be overnight successes, failing to show how much went into them in getting there. Unfortunately, this has built a certain laziness into us. We think we should be able to get everything really easily. But the world does not work that way. Tell me, can you show me a place in the world where a seed grows overnight into a magnificent redwood? Or where a tiny cub becomes a lion within a day? No, all great things will take time. And so will you.

Relentless

Kabir Bedi
Actor

Alyque would have these blinding flashes and insights on how a play should happen. You would perform it. He would keep chiselling away and make you do it differently. Then he would call in a team of friends who would see the revised version. Then they would have discussions, and he would get more ideas. Everything you had learnt was now rubbish. You would have to start all over again, building on a completely different premise with a completely different emotion underlying the words and the scene. It was sometimes frustrating as an actor, because once you've said something you are loathe to change it as you get comfortable with it. But Alyque would always push the boundaries, and he did brilliant things by the sheer dint of his hard work. I've never seen anyone more hardworking than Alyque. He kept working at it until he got it right; it didn't matter how many times in the process you had to relearn your lines or rethink your character's personality, tone or gestures. He would change everything and keep at it until he got it right. He didn't rest until he got the best possible solution, in anything he did. And that's what made the plays BRILLIANT.

The problem is that we have become too comfortable with our current way of being. And we don't challenge ourselves enough because we are worried about what people will say. To hell with it! Be persistent, provoke yourself and others. That will cause the true change in your life.

We have lost the ability to be persistent. Vandana tells me in neuroscience, they have discovered that 'neurons that wire together, fire together'.[1] Which means the more we practise something, the easier it becomes for us. And once we become used to doing that action, it becomes easier for us to make other changes too. So you have to practise being persistent at anything in order to build that persistence muscle inside you. So take up a new hobby—something you have always wanted to do—and work at it, whenever you can. I have countless examples of people who came into their element in their forties, fifties and sixties, so there's no doubt you can too. Actually it is not about age. It is just about keeping at it, even when it is boring and even when you want to give up. Just ask the actors in my plays about how many times I would get them to practise to get it right, every time.

I know it is even harder for the younger generation. But I want you and them to know that you have to keep at it if you want to get ahead!

When I joined the Cathedral school, in the first month, they were organizing a cross-country run. It seemed to me to be as long as a marathon, even though it was only three miles. I had never been in a race in my life. I was told it would be a cross-country run in the jungles. In those days, Jogeshwari in North Bombay, where they had planned it, was an absolute jungle.

But, ever willing to try, I said, 'OK,' and put my name down.

Now, that year we were told, 'We're not having it in Jogeshwari this year, we will use the maidan.' So that morning, we came out there, dressed in shorts and vests. It was damn cold. It was January. I looked around and I'd never seen so many boys competing! Unlike a jungle, where they would all be running in one direction, I slowly realized that we would all be able to see each other throughout the whole run.

The shot was fired and everyone started running. So, I started running, trying to keep up with the boys in front. We did the first round, then the second of the maidan and I was falling behind because I'd never run in my life. I'd had no training. By the time we came to the second maidan, I was half a maidan behind and my legs were killing me. By the time they finished the second maidan, I was a whole maidan behind.

Everyone was saying, 'Dropout! Dropout!' I didn't know what dropout even meant. The boys who had finished were given hot chocolate.

I was still running.

Can you imagine? Only me—there was no-one left. And I was hardly running. I was kind of walking-running, so tired that I could hardly breathe. Finally I finished, and when I came towards the medal table, the teachers had put up a tape for me. Most of the boys, however, were laughing at me. They'd finished their hot chocolate and biscuits. Many of them had driven off home, but some of them had stayed behind. Mainly to poke fun at me.

When I crossed the finishing line, the principal came up to me and said, 'Very well done. *It's not coming first but finishing the race that counts. You didn't drop out.*'

Two factors come into play: one is to have that determination, that if you start something you must finish it. And the second is that it has to be damn important for you that if you've started something, you need to finish it.

There is another secret about persistence. When you bring persistence into your life in one area, it is like magic: it spreads to other areas too. So if you are persistent in your conversations as an Agent Provocateur, you will find more and more answers will come your way. Don't give up!

'I Have No Special Talent. I Am Only Passionately Curious' [2]

This great quote by one of my heroes, Einstein, never ceases to inspire me. I think besides persistence, another hallmark of creativity is curiosity. I have always been relentlessly curious about everything, ever since I was little. I remember one of the things that made me more and more curious is when I observed one ant coming from one direction and hundreds of ants coming from a completely different direction. One ant would touch its antenna to the antennae of the other ants. And then it went on its way. I would make up stories about what the purpose could be. What information was it passing on and why did it have to do this? The idea of not knowing fascinated me and opened me up to explore.

I can look at anything and wonder endlessly about how it came to be. And by asking questions either to myself or others, it has often got me some glorious insights. For example, I have a painting in my flat from the great M.F. Hussain. I was doing *Othello* in 1990 in Mumbai. Kabir Bedi was Othello and I had a very good cast. Hussain, by chance, came to visit. A lightbulb sprung in my head and I immediately asked, 'Hussain sir, would you find it a challenge to do a poster for a play I'm doing?'

He said, 'Well, I'm going to London and I'm planning to sit for weeks and weeks at the Victoria and Albert Museum. So not at the moment, but perhaps when I get back.'

I said, 'No problem, but in your journeys to and from the museum, please take Shakespeare's *Othello* and read it there.' So off he went.

When he came back from London, he was positively excited. He said, 'What a fantastic story!'

I asked again, 'Will you do the poster?'

He said, 'Yes!'

He went back home. And the next morning he brought me this poster.

With childlike curiosity, I immediately wanted to know everything about it.

I asked, 'Why is there a yellow mask in Othello's hand?'

He said, 'Alyque, the way I see it, Othello treats his wife as a property, because he comes from a civilization apart. Originally, as Shakespeare says, he was a slave. Then he joined the Venetian army and became the general. He's a brilliant man. But in his heart, he grew up a slave. That's the reason he can't understand—very Indian in his attitude—that his wife is a person. To him, she is his property. So that's why she's the yellow mask: she's not a real person to him.'

Amazing.

Then there's a red image behind Othello. I asked Hussain, 'What is this?'

That's when he said, 'Ah, the red . . . that's Iago, who is poisoning our fellow's mind. He is a master manipulator, and he is very much like a puppeteer in the story. In every scene, Iago pushes Othello more and more to believe this story that his wife is unfaithful.'

I like being curious about everything. It gives me deep insights.

What are you missing in your life by not being curious? What are you just taking for granted?

And when you put together persistence and curiosity, just watch what modern alchemy you can do in your life.

Joy

You know, I have always gone into life with joy in my heart. I think the only way to get great solutions is to tackle them with joy in your heart. Worrying about solutions is not my idea of getting good solutions. You end up with boring solutions. Actually, if you are fearful about doing anything, then Vandana tells me that your amygdala gets active. It's the part of the brain responsible for the flight or fight response.[3] Now, a lesser-known fact is that when your amygdala gets triggered, norepinephrine and cortisol are released, causing your centre for growth and learning to shut down, which is why people often go numb when they are afraid.[4]

The other way to deal with finding solutions is tackling whatever you are facing with joy. When you do this, your prefrontal cortex has different neurotransmitters (including dopamine) which help bring in 'good vibes' and that calms you down.[5] If you worry all the time, you let your amygdala be hijacked, and that just brings you into animal 'freeze-flight-fright' mode. That's why in recent years, mindfulness and meditation have become so popular, as it has been found to engage your prefrontal cortex of the brain. Although it is not for me, Vandana swears by it. According to her and others, in as little as eight weeks, your grey matter starts to increase in density.[6] As a result, your whole 'being' calms down and you are able to look at your life more objectively. You feel joy and gratitude and realize how much you have to be grateful for.

Joy and Passion

Arshad Warsi
Actor

The commitment that Alyque has towards his work is phenomenal. I've never seen anybody like that. Very rarely do you come across people who are full of joy in their work—you know, they love what they do so much that they go to any length to get it right. It's just too much passion. It's hard to keep up with him and the level of dedication he has to do what he does. It's really difficult to keep up with that. You always feel you are not giving as much as he is giving. That is something that I really learnt from him. And if I ever reach a stage where I have to direct a film or play, that's one thing that I'm going to try to do: be more dedicated than anybody else on the set.

When you live life with joy, you are willing to take more risks as you know you will somehow make it work. My social work was all about bringing joy and abundance to other people, instead of them living in darkness through being ostracized. You could look at trying to help the Dalit movement in India as a thankless task, or you could choose to do something about it and make a difference.

Think about the examples I gave in the chapter on edutainment. Both Q and Shazahn panicked about their respective subjects in school—Q with maths and Shazahn with Hindi. They hated them. But when they found a new perspective to look at their subjects, it brought joy to them. And their knowledge bloomed.

Now would you rather be hijacked with fear or with joy?

Tricks

Here are some illustrated Alyqueisms that give you ideas to think differently, accompanied by a mishmash of stories to bring them alive.

Batteries Do Not Ignite

Vandana once said to me, 'You know Alyque, you're like a battery. I get recharged when I spend time with you. And so does everyone else.'

A compliment right?

Well, I got very cross. I told her emphatically, 'No, I am not like a battery at all.'

She looked at me quite worried, trying to figure out what was wrong.

I burst into a hearty laugh and raised an eyebrow. In my deepest voice, I said, 'I, my dear, am a magnetizer. I magnetize people, so they can go away and become magnets themselves. And share that magnetism with everyone they meet.'

She got it immediately.

I never want to be considered as a battery or glue or anything like that. And neither should you. Remember, a battery will wear out. Glue may be strong for a while, but over time it will dry and become brittle, and everything it kept together will fall apart.

I am most definitely a magnet.

Strive to create magnetism in your life. It will ensure you have the right people around you, who are drawn to you and match with your current. Then energize and empower them in such a way that they carry away your current and magnetize a whole generation of others.

Vandana tells me, 'That's what all of your friends and acquaintances say. You don't just empower a person, you ignite them into action.'

I ask her what impact I have had on her. The theme is the same. She looks up and says, 'Let's go through what happens. I come and meet you. You talk about an idea. I'm suddenly racing and I think to myself, "Oh my goodness, I never thought about that. Just think of the implications of a five-year marriage licence. Just think of all the happiness that getting rid of the hypocrisies will bring." And just that is enough to kick off my new thought processes.'

And that's what I want all of you to go through. I wanted to break down these ideas in a simple but entertaining way, so as to ignite you.

I now want you to turn up the heat on the flame, so that you combust those old thoughts and fry up new ones, turning into a magnetic, new you.

Inspire to Be Admired

Just that.

There's absolutely no point in putting any more down here. If you want to be admired, then find ways to inspire other people, don't just do run-of-the-mill stuff. Be a thought leader. Be bold and audacious. And most importantly, walk the talk.

Think of People, Not Their Robes

Many people I meet are intimidated by me. I haven't even spoken to them, and they are tongue-tied or nervous.

But actually, it is not me that they are nervous of: It is my position or what they see me as.

People have been like this with Vandana too. She left the UK for Romania at twenty-six, sold her first company when she was twenty-eight, has run the international division of a listed company, opening businesses all across Eastern Europe, then to top it off, is one of the youngest Asian women to have been honoured with an OBE from Her Majesty the Queen of England. Yet she's one of the most down-to-earth people I know. But others, before they meet her, are sometimes on guard.

People are like that with all sorts of people with titles and uniforms, like with the police, doctors and senior government officials.

We seem to forget that they are all just people inside. They were born like you and me.

They are all just human.

Even a police commissioner will get up in his pyjamas. And he has his breakfast in his pyjamas, maybe. He goes to the toilet just like you and me. *But*, as soon as he puts on that uniform, your whole attitude to him and his life changes. Remember though, that one minute he is petting his dog at home, maybe one of his nieces or nephews rings him up and he's a very different person. But in the office, he assumes the robes and therefore the role of someone else.

It is the robes that make him powerful.

But there is nothing to be frightened of.

In *Tughlaq*, Girish Karnad's fantastic play, there was a lot of scandal about my opening scene (which I inserted with Girish's permission). Kabir Bedi, who played Tughlaq, is almost nude with his back to the audience. And then two servants come forward and start dressing him in front of the audience. Eventually they dress him and put on his pagri and he turns to the audience and he just stares. He is an ordinary, simple, bare, forked animal (as Shakespeare said), and then suddenly he is the emperor.

The robes make him the emperor. And I forget who said that it is the gowns or the robe that make you who you are.

That's all. So don't let the robes fool you.

They are all just human beings underneath—just remember that.

Don't Retire but Re-tyre

There is a large stratum of society that is growing in population every day, and it's getting bigger and bigger. Quite honestly, if they are not needed, or don't feel needed, we are going to have the biggest depressed adult generation on our hands. People are always talking about the millennials and Gen Z, but they are not talking about the other generations enough.

The bigger problem is not education at the bottom.

It's a problem at the top.

The population of over fifty-fives is mushrooming, and most of our Indian ones simply don't know what to do with themselves.

That's why I talk about a second innings.

Unfortunately, we seem to think that learning new skills is mainly for the younger ones and only at school and university. Many people in their fifties and sixties are not thinking about learning anything new. Conventional wisdom (and the law in some places) says that you retire at the age of sixty or sixty-five. Some countries have increased it and may increase it again, as the longevity of the human being increases. Yet even if the government does, it is increasingly harder to get a job as you get older.

It is frustrating though, for those people approaching retirement. The management of organizations are not thinking, 'Hey, wait a minute. We're dealing with a human being here. S/he is fit and healthy at sixty, thanks to medicines and sport. We're letting go of one of our best assets, just because a law made it up that they must retire at sixty.'

Then at sixty, most people will still be looking at a lifespan of up to ninety minimum, maybe a hundred. Now if you talk about a healthy person, really, what are you going to do from sixty to ninety? That's thirty years, or forty years to one hundred!

Ultimately, you've got the second half of your life to live. And this makes people very depressed, as they are faced with a lot of uncertainty. After they leave their employment or business, the retired people realize that their life is not over, but everything that kept them so busy has now gone. That's the main thing. There's a tremendous sense of lack and emptiness. As long as you are needed, you feel loved. When you're not needed, you feel unloved, and that is a very depressing thing. Newly retired people suddenly become personae non grata at home. Whereas in the office, they were respected and considered senior, no one treats them like that at home. Everyone else has their own life and is busy getting on with it.

I know when I retired, although I had consultancies already in hand, I missed the whole ambience of working together with other people. It took me some time to adjust to being a consultant, which is really an individual who works for a group, but not on a permanent basis or with a permanent team.

So I think you have to prepare people for that.

And that's why I say don't retire, but *re-tyre*. Put another tread on your tyre. Your tyre is in good condition. It is only the tread that is worn out.

There are so many people who are frustrated at that retirement age. They are so fixated on what is going wrong in their lives now that they have quite forgotten the dreams that they had given up when they were young and free. This is the perfect time to reconnect with those, and in so doing, give back to others!

There are closet singers, painters and musicians, and people who, for example, wanted to be a musician, but there were no openings when they were young. Now they are old, they could consider training younger people and get the joy of nurturing the talent that they never got a chance to practise.

When I run these seminars for retired people, they often bring their spouses. And when I give this talk, at the end, it is always the women who raise their hands and say, 'Thank you, because now I won't have him sitting on my head telling me how to cook, how to run the garden, how to clean the house. I will have myself back as the boss. And he will be running his own little outfit, whatever it is, as his boss.'

Also, remember, as you get older, your body starts to degenerate. You know, the bones begin to creak, your digestion also goes for a six and then life becomes a tedious, boring thing. But the mind will not accept that. Yet, the body has to. Your legs are paining but you have to walk. Growing old is a challenge. It is not easy to accept. I still refuse to accept that I'm growing old.

By re-tyring, you forget about what's going on inside your body and concentrate on what makes you happy.

The Magic of Re-tyring Early

Boman Irani
Actor

Back in the day, I was a photographer, and as a photographer, I had just started getting some work. I just started paying my bills and I just started getting my life back on track. Things weren't good before that. I had met Shiamak Davar, and he was the first celebrity who got some pictures done with me.

One day he came and told me, 'I'm taking you for lunch.'

I said, 'All right, let's go,' thinking to myself, hey, a free lunch!

But he doesn't. He takes me to a building called Christmas Eve instead. I don't even know what's in that lane—I thought there was a restaurant up there. And he takes me up to the third floor.

I said, 'This is a residential building.

He said, 'Yeah.'

I said, 'Where are you taking me?'

'I'm taking you for an audition. Sing a song.'

I started singing a song as I knocked on the door, and this lady opens the door. We go in and there's Alyque sitting in the distance. I walk straight back out of the apartment in the Christmas Eve building, and I tell Shiamak, 'What have you brought me here for?'

'For an audition. I want you to act in a play.'

I said, 'You must be joking. I've just about gotten my act together. I'm just about paying my bills. I don't want to be an actor. It's the wrong time.'

So, he says, 'This is, believe me, this is the right time.'

I said, 'I'm not an actor.'

He replied, 'Says who?'

I didn't have an answer to that, because in my heart, always, I always wanted to be on stage.

So he says, 'Don't lie to me. Don't lie to yourself.'

And he took me to meet Alyque. Alyque sat there and Shiamak and he had a long discussion because at that point, Shiamak was going to do the choreography. Then Alyque said, 'Who's this?'

Shiamak said, 'He's a photographer called Boman Irani. He's going to sing for you.'

Alyque was OK with that, and I sang for him. He immediately cast me in a very important role, within all of four or five minutes. So Alyque put me to the grind on that production. And then he got me involved in moving around in the crowd and then with lifting furniture. Then he got me involved with writing bits and the rest, as they say, is history.

Cross Pollination Is the Key to Healthy Growth

This is something that people don't do enough of, or simply don't know how to do. If I ask you to think of the people you turn to in a crisis or difficulty, will you find that most of those people are from the same socio-economic background, age, religion and culture as you? I bet most of them are.

My friend, you are living in an echo chamber.

Diversity is what keeps our world alive. And we are rapidly falling towards DIE-versity.

The most successful people I know are the ones who keep wide circles of friends and get information from different places. Most people don't—when they go to an event, they stick with their own clique or someone introduced by the clique.

When you're at a cocktail party, if you are making the most of it in AP style, you may meet a banker, a professor, a scientist. It's wonderful, because you flit from conversation to conversation like a butterfly or bee with flowers, picking up bits and pieces from each person. The variety of it is so lovely that you should make an effort to talk to as many different people as you can, *as it ends up breeding a new variety of ideas in you.*

A lot of these ideas actually found their way into practice when I ran Lintas. I was given a totally free hand, adjusting the entire atmosphere and the structure and everything as long as I delivered a profit. And I knew one key would be exposing my team to people that they would not normally meet, or to ideas that they would not normally hear about.

So, one of the things I introduced at Lintas was a lunchtime stimulation session, where I would invite someone not directly related to our field, for example, M.F. Hussain to give a talk. Or a poet or someone from science, so that there would be a melting pot of ideas in everyone's heads. They would take some of those as ingredients and cook up an ingenious new recipe in their next ad. People would really enjoy it.

If you want ingenious ideas, then cook your mind with diversity as your chief ingredient.

Tools

Throughout my life, I have invented many systems that work for me. And I want to share three of them with you. Two are real ones I have used. The third is an invented tool that I would love to see in existence.

OICA

I always found business school topics very useful. But some of them didn't go far enough for me. For example, SWOTs (strengths, weaknesses, opportunities and threats framework). This business school favourite doesn't really help you find a direction to go in; it simply lists what you know about yourself.

I invented something called OICA—it is a giant leap from the SWOT. It's a simple way with which anyone can find a creative solution to any challenge facing them.

OICA stands for:

O—Observation
I—Insight out of the observation
C—Conceptualization of a solution
A—Actualization of a solution

To show you how it works, let's take a simple example. How can we come up with a more thrilling and interesting version of the long five-day test match cricket that will appeal to a larger audience?

Using OICA, we would do the following.

Ask the question, 'What is wrong with cricket at the moment?'

The Observation would be that cricket is a boring game and it is likely to die out. It takes five days and everyone dresses in white as if they are going to some birth ceremony or wedding (in the West) or a funeral (in India). It is very slow—five days. In this day and age, people can't sit still doing the same thing for five days! And the rules are convoluted.

The Insight is based on the question, 'What are the problems with that for the viewer?'

Well, test match cricket is based on who has the most wickets in hand. You know the game. So if West Indies is playing New Zealand, if West Indies scores 300 runs in the first innings and 300 runs in the second innings and New Zealand scores only 200 runs in the first innings, if in the second innings on the fifth day New Zealand still has three wickets in hand at close, it's a draw.

How can it be a draw after five whole days? West Indies whipped New Zealand!

The insight therefore is: test match cricket is based on the wrong premise.

The premise of all games is that whoever scores the most in a certain timespan wins. Applying this same logic to test match cricket, with a five-day time slot, whoever scores the most runs should win.

What if we turned cricket into football? Football is about how many goals you score. Even if you saved one hundred goals and score a single goal, it's the scored goals that count. That is the answer. Turn cricket into football.

So, in order to increase the number of people watching, you have to have a shorter time limit, let's say one day. Now we're beginning to develop the Concept. It was based on the insight that cricket should be based on the number of runs you make in a time period, not the number of wickets you have lost. Conceptualization would be coming up with a system for playing cricket where you had a winner within one day.

The final Actualization is the rules drawn up for one-day cricket. And why do you have to wear white, why can't you wear colours? So let's have colourful uniforms for fun, like football jerseys, worshipped all over the world. And get cheerleaders like in American football. Let's give the crowd a little more excitement. This eventually happened with the twenty-over cricket format.

What you have done is hijack a boring, conventional sport and 'OICA-ed' it into a multi-billion-dollar enterprise, filled with thrill and excitement, totally relevant to today's audience.

Basically OICA can be applied to almost anything. OICA is something that you can use to add to your ability to solve challenges.

With OICA, you see the world as upside down, and you'll get a fresh perspective on it. This is the way I know and think. The concept turns the world upside down, and the actualization is a new way to do something. All my creativity gives you a fresh perspective on whatever it may be. In marriage, I will give you a fresh perspective; in terrorism, I will give you a fresh perspective. Take terrorism for example. If you observe, everybody says the only way to deal with the terrorists is catch them and kill them. The insight is that there are other, religiously acceptable ways to deal with terrorists: excommunicate them because they rely on a religion. Pull the rug from under their feet. Say they're not religious at all, they are the opposite of religious and that gives them a jolt. And then use the rest of OICA to come up with the excommunication orders.

People think in straight lines. That's unhelpful. Find a different way of thinking and you will find a different way in life. You need to think in squiggly lines.

It's somewhere around there, where you will get a fresh and valuable perspective.

AP's Magical Filing System

I have always had people ask me, 'Alyque, how do you find time to do all the things you do? From advertising to theatre, to social causes and nurturing others?'

Do I have a magic trick?

No, only a great support ecosystem and a methodical note-taking and filing system.

When I was at Lintas, I had some great secretaries, Anne Sequeira and Lalita D'Silva. And, of course, Ida, my housekeeper. They have been the people who helped me do what I needed to do and not have to worry about everyday mundane tasks.

My filing system was legendary. Every time someone needed something from me, I would instruct them to put it in a folder. I had a folder for the month, then one for other projects I would do over the year. Each week, they would dutifully pull out of the system what I needed for that week. Anything I didn't do was filed meticulously, for the following week or the month. That way, I didn't miss anything.

I would also always have a pencil and a notepad with me, wherever I went. Any time I thought of something that I wanted to do or heard something interesting, I would note it down. Then at the end of the day, I would have a call with Anne or Lalita and work out where to file it. They would slot it into the relevant file.

At home, I had several cabinets which would have the names of the projects I was working on. Vandana has a drawer all to herself. Any time I found something relevant, I would stick it in that folder, and before she would come to visit, I would go through the documents and pass the information on to her. Ida, my housekeeper, knew these drawers intimately and so she could help me find anything if the others were not around.

Anne and Lalita would also keep lists of whichever events I was speaking at and the content of those speeches. If I was invited to a new place, I could see my notes from previous speaking engagements to see if there were similarities. This cut down my preparation time considerably.

It sounds simple, but it required a great deal of dedication to keep the system going. I am a stickler for organization and would get quite annoyed if I could not find anything, so that kept everyone on their toes. Persistence, persistence, persistence!

Vandana is far more modern than me. She has a brilliant system with her executive assistant, the ever efficient Glenda Watsa. Vandana does not believe in to-do lists. She, like me, notes things down and Glenda immediately diarizes when she is going to do something. Her diary is colour coded in all sorts of colours so she knows what she is doing and when.

So organization is key, but the use of the information in that organizational system is more important. The right system can turn your thoughts into alchemy.

Note-Taking the AP Way

Ronnie Screwvala

For the last thirty years, I have had this format of the pad, which I designed back then and is modelled on AP's pad. It's one of the early habits I picked up from AP—I was pretty young, and early impressions stay with you. I remember he would always have a notepad on his office table. It had a distinctive style—with a from, to and date. He was always sending out notes to people, because at that time there was no internet or WhatsApp. That's a habit that stuck with me. I designed the pad thirty years ago and it's become a patent for what I do, but it's come from AP.

Business Clubs

I thought of this forty years ago, but I never pursued this framework. It's an audacious one and will take some doing if it is implemented in real life. I was on a committee run by the then governor's wife, and we were talking about Gandhi and that during his life, he altered his views about many things—caste being one of them. Towards the end of his life, he expressed his desire to abolish the caste system.[7]

It takes time to extract such a strong ideology from the brain. And it is going to take a long time before people will truly accept that it is a system which openly discriminates, trying to put people in boxes that they cannot come out of because of the prejudices of those boxes. Until we can get people to look beyond caste and see human beings for what they are, it will always be difficult, so we need to find ways for people to get to know each other again, in a way that does not breed inequality. So, I came up with one such idea. I said to that committee, 'Look, you can't abolish something without having something else in its place. People will be lost. So, if you want to abolish the caste system, you will have to replace it with something, as *people like to belong*.'

This is a very nature-inspired idea. A seed needs many elements to be able to become a tree—water, sunlight, nutrients and so on. It needs variety. Human beings are no less. There's a certain strength and a certain variety if we are to grow in what we love to do, so I feel, why don't we have one replacement for the 'caste system' based on clubs? Like Vandana's UK India Business Group. If you ever go there, you'd be bored unless you liked to talk about Indo–UK business. If you love cricket, why not have a cricket club, where they only talk and play cricket? Those could be a new way of creating belonging.

See, if you have homogenous interests, the chances are others will all share the same attitude that you do towards life, like lawyers, doctors and businessmen generally do. Unlike having something that you were born with and can't change. This is where you can say, 'This is not forced on me. I was not born into this, where I can't change it; I can change.'

If I'm a doctor and I love music and I know many doctors who do, you would have a club for them. But, at a later age, maybe fifty or sixty, if you want to be a musician you're entitled to change clubs. And why not belong to different clubs at the same time?

It is to do with your skills, rather than your birth right.

There is always the danger that if all the businesspeople are in the same club, then their thinking is going to get homogenized just like a caste. But then you have to say, 'OK, we're getting homogenized, ideas are the same, so let's invite people to disrupt our mindsets.' I have always believed in disruption—it leads to cross-pollination.

Being Hijacked

From the View of Siddharth Roy Kapoor
Founder and Managing Director, Roy Kapur Films

I grew up idolizing Alyque and his 'double life' in theatre and advertising. For a kid obsessed with the idea of being involved in the movies and the theatre while still yearning for the financial security that a steady job would provide, he was my first glimpse of someone who had been able to meld their passions with their talents into one cohesive, creatively fulfilling and financially viable whole—to have their cake and to eat it too! He was the god of advertising by day and lorded over the world of theatre by night. What could be better!

But it was only when I worked for him as an actor in his productions of *Final Solutions* and *Evita* that I got a front row seat to how he actually did it. His punishing work ethic, his attention to detail, his rigour and discipline and—what might seem contradictory to these qualities but what made him so unique—his disregard for the tried and tested, his embrace of popular culture, his fascination with contemporary times, his refusal to rest on nostalgia and to never muse wistfully about 'the way things were' but to always look ahead with optimism. The man had a passion for life and an urge to make every minute count. He was always 'the youngest person in the room' when it came to his hunger to learn as much as he could about the current zeitgeist and for his ability to cast off the shackles of conventional social mores.

I am so fortunate to have had the privilege of working with him closely, to have been able to observe both his amazing creative process and his genius for people management. My experience with Alyque has informed the way I look at the world, has helped me wholeheartedly embrace all it has to offer and has inspired me to believe you really can have it all if you want it badly enough, are willing to work hard enough and have resolved to never, never give up. There will never be another AP.

I hope you have got some ideas from this chapter. They are quite simple ideas and if you apply them to your life, you will find that life will look brighter and be enriched. Isn't that what we really want and are looking for, deep down?

Extracting the Essence

- Provoke others and yourself, and get ready for new fountains of thought.
- Be relentless.
- Curiosity generates learning.
- Aim to magnetize, not ignite.
- Inspire to be admired.
- Go beyond the robes, to the person.
- Cross-pollination is the key to holistic creation.

Hijacking your Mind—Points for You to Ponder

- Where do you not poke yourself?
- What do you give up on too easily?
- What industries do you know nothing about? How can you meet people from there and swap ideas?

14

The New Ten Commandments

This above all; to thine own self be true.

—*Hamlet*, Act I, Scene III

I really feel we need a modern-day leader, like Jesus Christ or Mahatma Gandhi, to rethink, 'Why are we on this earth? What is our purpose, and if there is no purpose, how should we live our lives?'

In the present world, we only think of ourselves. I exist and no one else does. We have become standard, self-centred individuals who only think of our own gain, and usually, a material gain. And it should really be that the world is one huge joint family. We have lost sight of that.

If you are not a caring and sharing human being, then you are not serving a purpose. The reason for why you were put in this world. I don't think we are here just for our nuclear or extended family. I think we are here for the people around us, who may need us. You may feel you are too busy to help them. But are you at least thinking about them? It is a well-known fact that thought eventually leads to action.

But 'eventually' sometimes takes a long time . . .

In Chapter 3, I mention the new joint family. I used my own example. But the idea behind that was, why can't we live as friends instead of enemies? Why is everyone always comparing themselves with others, comparing with neighbours—he has something and I don't, therefore I don't like him . . .?

While religion is supposed to give us guidelines or principles, we have turned these into unbreakable rules, which is rather silly and doesn't fit our present day.

So I decided to rewrite the Ten Commandments, Alyque Padamsee style. I don't care if God wrote the original Ten Commandments—he won't mind that I have used the idea and changed them about a bit, for current times.

    I   Thou shalt treat all human beings as equal.
   II Thou shalt speak out when thou seest injustice.
  III Thou shalt help thy neighbour in need.
  IV Thou shalt shun dishonesty.
   V Thou shalt respect thy neighbour's religion.
  VI Thou shalt build bridges, not barriers.
 VII Thou shalt not practise double standards.
VIII Thou shalt always respect women.
  IX Thou shalt not blame the many for the sins of the few.
   X Thou shalt always listen to the voice of thy conscience.

Why don't you have a go at writing your own Ten Commandments? I promise you, it won't be as easy as you think. But when you have them and really live by them, your life will never be the same.

15

Hacking Your Life

Key Messages and Bigger
Questions from Each Chapter

If you have got this far, then I hope you are well and truly hijacked.

So, what do you do if you really want to take this book to heart?

1) Think about which chapters make you feel uncomfortable and have a chat with yourself about it. Is it because you vehemently disagree, or are old norms forcing you away from freedom?
2) Have one-on-one conversations with people about each chapter—discuss the 'protocol prisons' that we live in and get each other to make up your own minds about why you do it. Remember, these are MY thoughts—be clear about your own thoughts on each of these topics, instead of living with the voices of the past.
3) Volunteer! I learnt so much about life through social causes. Get involved with a cause close to your heart and make a difference.
4) Each one reach one. There are billions who 'have not'. As a bonus baby, which individual can you take on to truly support?

Is there a maid's daughter that you can chat with on a regular basis, to advise, mentor and coach? What difference would it make to her life? And to yours?

5) Speak up! Write about the nonsense that we are still following on social media and get the conversation going with strangers and friends. Get involved with conversations that others start on these topics too.

It's time to revisit each of the chapters with a little Alyque Padamsee twist. If you are game, do answer these and share some of your answers on social media with #askalyque.

1.   I would never sleep with a stranger

We are all hypocrites at some time or the other. It's natural. But isn't it time to stop the hypocrisies that just don't have room in the world today?

Ahem, what about you? What hypocrisy are you continuing to perpetuate? Where are you being a modern slave to the cacophonic ghosts of the past? Those friends you keep in touch with but don't excite you anymore? Your job? Your partner?

DO SOMETHING ABOUT IT! You can and you must, if you are going to make this world a better place.

2.   The union of taxpayers who refuse to pay tax

The Hindi expression *Paisa Vasool* (value for money) is so important to all of us in India. Yet, do we demand it from our government? We may count the rupees, but there are billions going down the drain.

What are your intrinsic gifts that are going down the drain because you are involved with other stuff? Why aren't you giving yourself time to flourish? If you are good at writing, why aren't you publishing more? If singing, why aren't you joining more online competitions? If acting, then join the theatre, dammit!

What can you make yourself accountable for, which will put pure joy in your 'happiness bank account'?

3. Do you need a licence to marry your partner?

This chapter is not just about a marriage licence and whether marriage as a concept should be rethought.

It is about asking you to rethink yourself.

What aspects of your life do you refuse to put an expiry date on? Well, let me tell you, you are already past your sell-by date, if you don't think about it.

Choose three areas of your life that need to be renewed. It could be your relationship, your job or even your weight. How can you make a deal with yourself to improve these areas? Renew a 'licence' for self-development. That will keep you on your toes and bring you violent happiness!

4. Ten for men (and zero for everyone else)

Do you really believe in equality and equity? Do you realize that women have had it bad for centuries, nay, millennia? It is time to come on the field to support women and not sit on the sidelines.

But where have you not given yourself the best chance to succeed at something? You went to the gym but didn't get a trainer? You got a new assignment, but made no effort to find someone who could help you understand what was needed?

We all have areas of ourselves that need to be healed. It could be a 'generations-old' trauma. So identify it and solve it, so future generations don't have to deal with it.

5. Make way for the C?O instead of the CEO

We all want to live in a happy world. Given that we spend so much time with work-related people in our organizations, shouldn't we make it more like a family, instead of being in compartments, like a newspaper?

So, what can you do that will transform the atmosphere with the people that you work and spend time with? What C?O role can you play? And what impact will it have?

6. Change the battlefield: Selling the truth

What are you selling and to whom? Which emotions? And what do they buy in return? How do you massage your messages to them? And how are you massaged in return?

7. School versus edutainment

I really pity the young ones at school today. What can we do to make life better for them? If everyone reading this book rewrote just one part of the curriculum, we would have such an amazing schooling system!

What curriculum are you running internally inside your head that is old and outdated? What should be thrown out and reinvented inside you? How can you do it?

8. Repaying the accident of birth

How do you change lives?

I don't mean give to charity and all that, I mean actually talk to another human being and change their life? You know you have multiple opportunities a day to do it. It may be speaking to the society handy man, security guard or maid. It may be taking a real interest in their lives and helping them sort out something, helping them learn something new, or try something new. Just being around them in a positive manner may make the difference.

You are the change. Can you hurry up and be it now?

9. Why are terrorists breaking the law of their very own holy book?

Look, this isn't about the terrorists per se. Aren't we all terrorists many times a day, in fact, Kamikaze bombers blowing up ourselves and those we love around us?

By not following their own spiritual teachings, the religious extremists are in fact hurting the very people they have sworn to protect: their fellow Muslims. And of course, themselves.

Where are you self-sabotaging?

Where are you saying one thing and doing another? It might be about mending a relationship or learning a skill that you are not making time for.

10. I speak to God every night. Pity you can't

You don't need to go through somebody to talk to God. It's more about you going through your thoughts to find the real you. You seem to believe everything you think is true. Well, it is not.

It's time you took ownership and accountability for your WHOLE life, not cherry-pick only what you want to do. Stop having conversations with others and start having conversations with yourself.

Another point. Instead of blindly following your faith, why not look at the *principles* that faith is trying to imbue and focus on them instead? Don't look at who lived where and what they said to each other. Take the lesson they wanted to impart and live that as your truth.

What truth are you not dealing with? What are you refusing to accept about yourself? Who do you rely on to tell you what to do? And why don't you take responsibility for yourself in certain areas? The world is all about life-long learning, and you will find you have the answers if you ask yourself the questions you're too scared to.

11. Speaking the unspoken dialogues

If only we could listen to what people are thinking in their heads. We might be able to deal with a lot of pain. People's heads have become like ever-swelling balloons with thoughts being pushed in from everywhere. They're stretching and stretching but are getting to the point where they will pop and explode.

But speaking your innermost thoughts to someone is like putting a strip of sticky tape on the surface of the balloon and then sticking a pin in it. You will deflate softly and easily, and when you get to a point where you are comfortable again, you can re-seal your brain balloon.

What should you get off your chest? What secrets are weighing you down more than gravity on Jupiter? And why won't you do something about it?

Just remember that when you do, you will be so much lighter. And that lightness will ignite the people around you. It might even encourage some of your friends to do the same. Just try it.

12. My one thousand best friends

Who are your thousand best friends? I bet pretty soon some characters from serials on TV or Netflix will come up—you know them better than members of your own extended family. Admit it!

If your life is a theatre production where you play the main character, what would it show? Who would be in it?

If you had a play reading with the audience, what would they say?

Isn't it time you spent less time picking apart other relationships or news in a part of the world you have no influence over, and start picking apart your life?

Be curious, not fearful. Be the detective in your life. There has been no crime committed—the detective is there to work out how to make your life even better!

13. Smart Alyque's tips, tricks and tools for a hijacked life

What are your smart hacks? What works for you?

Which tools and which chapters fascinated you the most? What would it take to bring them into your life? And what difference would it make?

And finally, you yourself are a tool. A tool that can bring about change. When will you wake up and realize that you have the potential and can maximize it too?

14. The New Ten Commandments

At this stage, if you have had a go at answering some of the questions, can you put together your Ten Commandments? And try living by them? See what it does to your life. And then answer this question:

What else is there left to HIJACK?

Now, my co-mates and brothers in exile,
Hath not old custom made this life more sweet
Than that of painted pomp?
Are not these woods
More free from peril than the envious court?
Here feel we not the penalty of Adam,

The seasons' difference, as the icy fang
And churlish chiding of the winter's wind,
Which, when it bites and blows upon my body,
Even till I shrink with cold, I smile and say,
'This is no flattery. These are counselors
That feelingly persuade me what I am.'
Sweet are the uses of adversity,
Which, like the toad, ugly and venomous,
Wears yet a precious jewel in his head.
And this our life, exempt from public haunt,
Finds tongues in trees, books in the running brooks,
Sermons in stones, and good in everything.

                              —*As You Like It*, Act II, Scene I

Afterword

Vandana Saxena Poria

The phone rang.

It was my executive assistant, Glenda. She was in a panic.

'Kiki Watsa (Premila Lal) is having a lunch and wants you to be there. She thinks your OBE could be of interest for the guest she has over for lunch.'

I laughed. Nobody says no to Kiki Watsa (Premila Lal, Glenda's larger than life mother-in-law and well-known author of India's original cookbooks). I didn't even ask who the guest was. I just said yes.

And there began one of the most audacious adventures of my life.

The guest was none other than Padmashree Alyque Padamsee. Even though I had grown up in the UK, I knew this name well. Not just because of his advertising career and theatre life, which most people in India knew him for. But because he had played Jinnah in Attenborough's *Gandhi*. I had seen it when I was younger, and the film had a profound impact on me.

So now I was going to lunch with him and his two daughters, Raëll and Shazahn.

I did my homework. Aside from being an absolute living legend in theatre, advertising and social work, he also had this multi-talented family of ex-wives and children who were all making waves in their respective fields.

And countless protégés. From Shiamak Davar to Dalip Tahil to Kabir Bedi to Sabira Merchant to Ronnie Screwvala. He made India proud—on a global stage.

So, as you can imagine, I was intrigued to meet the man who had been an inspiration and guide to all of these icons. From my work on mindset, I knew how heavily your family members influence you, much more so than you consciously realize.

I got there early, and Kiki was fussing over last-minute arrangements. I then heard a bellowing voice. 'Kiki Watsa, my darling, how are you, you old chestnut? Have you been a good girl? I bloody well hope not!' Followed by a hearty laugh.

I was in shock. No one I know had the courage to talk to Kiki that way. But she giggled like a schoolgirl and gave him a bear hug. The closeness and warmth of this fraternity was something to be marvelled at.

I have to say that even though I have met royalty and many other celebrities on countless occasions, this man had an inexorable charm about him. Whether it was his voice or grand gestures, I was immediately curious to know more about the way his mind worked.

When we finally sat down at the table, he looked at me and said, 'So, Madam Vandana, tell me about yourself.'

I told him about my youth in the UK, becoming a chartered accountant instead of a DJ, my ten years in Eastern Europe with a start-up, selling out to a listed company and the past decade in India in the business world. I told him about my love of bringing people and organizations together, with my work at Common Purpose, the UK–India Business Council and the Institute of Chartered Accountants. And I told him about my unquenchable thirst for understanding why people are the way they are, networking dynamics and how they can make big changes happen that benefit the masses. He wanted to know everything, especially about my children, Jai and Zara. Years later, he told me that he felt he had been a neglectful father and never once failed to ask me how my children were doing in our meetings or calls.

But the thing that bonded us was when I told him about the series of visionary novels that I was writing. They include other worlds, where men were not the decision makers. He was particularly taken aback when I told him of a female-centric planet I had developed, where women are the dominant force.

He laughed a deep, hearty laugh as I described how it worked—very different from our planet. 'I like your thinking. I like that you have challenged something that is taken as gospel. Turned the world on its head. My, my, I would never have taken you for a chartered accountant. You should have been in advertising. Tell me more . . .'

And there began a beautiful friendship.

At the end of the lunch, he asked me to come to Mumbai to visit him to chat about life, the universe and everything. I agreed.

A few weeks later, I turned up at Christmas Eve, Alyque's home in Breach Candy. The amazing Ida, his housekeeper, had cooked us a wonderful lunch. And we just talked. We talked of politics, both Indian and global, his time in the UK, his children, his love for theatre, for social causes and his passion for advertising. He had a refreshing view on life and wasn't afraid to 'tell it how it is'. And he thought so differently about everything. We talked about 3D printing of body parts and brain transplants, about how life would have been if dinosaurs had still been around, the confusion of love and lust and how the world could be changed for the most downtrodden of global society. How offices should be run like extended families and how children could be encouraged to learn the most boring of topics in a way that they would enjoy.

I was fully charged—like a bolt of electricity had hit me. He had that effect on most people!

I really wanted to 'mine his mind' and understand why he thought like that—what and who had inspired his thinking. So, he graciously told me about his childhood, his influences from marching ants to Einstein, and of course his education (and hatred for the current system). He raved about his protégés who had become global stars and the others who had made their mark in India.

I visited him a few times over the next months, and the discussion was always scintillating. Anyone who has ever met AP will tell you that he tickles the mind, then wholeheartedly ignites it.

At one of our lunches, he said to me, 'You know Vandana, I wrote a book years ago. Well, I didn't write it, I had a collaborator Arun Prabhu who finally got it down. But that was years ago—it became a must-read at MBA schools. I think I have a book in me now. But I don't know how to get it out. I am a visual person and very good at talking, but I don't know what the hell this book is going to be about.'

'How about . . .' I said gingerly, 'I record our conversations over the next few times, and we see what themes come out?'

Over the next two to three years, I visited Alyque every few weeks. We talked and talked. We talked about his life, his regrets and his high points. He would send me notes through his secretary Anne Sequeira. He allowed me unfettered access to all his old speeches and all of his contacts, and I went with him to several of his speaking engagements and theatre readings. There I would see how loved he was, by all age groups. He really was a living legend in every sense of the word. Everywhere I went, I would take copious notes and recordings with different people, to find out what the elusive theme was to his life—the one he was looking for that would make the meat of this book.

Alyque would often phone me up with a crazy idea that we would argue about for sixty minutes and then agree to discuss later. Then we would do our recorded sessions, where I would poke him on everything he said. I would challenge him on something he said or ask him why he thought the way he did on various topics from the state of education to religion. I was always in a complete spin by the time I left, and his family told me that he was too. Somehow, we had this ability to push each other into reflecting on why we are the way we are at the deepest level.

The trouble was that there were so many themes! And I was getting mired in all the chaos that was Alyque Padamsee's brain. So, one day, Glenda and I got a big whiteboard and took down all the areas we had discussed over the years, the hundreds of pages of notes, to look for commonalities.

There it was.

He had a way of hijacking your mind.

He had this enviable gift of showing a completely different perspective on anything and everything, so you would expand your thinking and see new views of an old problem. And he saw all of them in glorious, technicolour detail. He also had a host of techniques to try to solve problems.

Alyque passed away before we could finish the book. But there was enough there on paper that he was happy with. We finalized all the chapter headings and the major parts of the content. He was absolutely insistent that this must be an uncomplicated short book that was written very simply and would be accessible to people all around the world, of any age. He knew his immediate fraternity would be aware of many of the ideas in this book, but he wanted it to reach a larger audience across the globe—especially the younger generation. He believes we have failed them, and their only hope for success is to get out of the thinking that has been handed down to them.

And the book you are reading is what he wanted to say to the world.

Human beings are fundamentally unhappy, within society, across the world. And that is because we have been conditioned into thinking that the rules that we have been brought up with are right.

And it is time to hijack our minds.

Any mistakes or errors in this book are entirely mine. I am grateful to the whole Padamsee family for giving me the opportunity to share this with you and I hope it does make you think differently. Because if we all did, we could change the world into a more equitable and inclusive place.

Alyque, I hope you are up there amongst the stars, partying away and putting on plays for the powers that be. And I hope I have done you justice.

Notes

Introduction

1. Volatility, uncertainty, complexity and ambiguity.

Chapter 1

1. See https://www.prsindia.org/parliamenttrack/vital-stats/profile-newly-elected-17th-lok-sabha.
2. See https://www.bbc.com/future/article/20190326-what-is-epigenetics.
3. Damon Centola, Joshua Becker, Devon Brackbill, Andrea Baronchelli, 'Experimental evidence for tipping points in social convention', *Science*, Vol. 360, Issue 6393, 2018, pages 1116 to 1119.

Chapter 2

1. See https://www.financialexpress.com/economy/how-many-people-in-india-actually-pay-tax-income-tax-department-clarifies-pm-modis-claim/1867332/.

Chapter 3

1. The Bible, Romans 7:2–3.
2. The Bible, 1 Corinthians 7:39.
3. See https://www.courts.ca.gov/1039.htm?rdeLocaleAttr=en.

Chapter 4

1. See https://www.cmie.com/kommon/bin/sr.php?kall=warticle&dt=2021-03-15%2018:34:14&msec=256.
2. See https://iwwage.org/womens-share-in-urban-labour-force-just-at-10-3-per-cent/.
3. See https://www.forbesindia.com/blog/coronavirus/why-covid-19-became-a-womens-problem-in-urban-india/ and https://www.grantthornton.in/globalassets/1.-member-firms/india/assets/pdfs/women-in-business-2021.pdf.
4. See https://www.reuters.com/article/us-india-rape-caste-idUSKBN28509J.
5. Alison Bechdel from 'The Rule' (Comic strip, 'Dykes to watch out for', 1985).
6. Victim's statement to the police, https://www.dnaindia.com/mumbai/report-mumbai-gang-rape-full-text-of-the-victims-statement-to-the-police-1880031.
7. DNA, Pune edition, 26 January 2014, p. 1.
8. S354 Indian Penal Code. Assault or criminal force to woman with intent to outrage her modesty. —Whoever assaults or uses criminal force to any woman, intending to outrage or knowing it to be likely that he will thereby outrage her modesty, shall be punished with imprisonment of either description for a term which may extend to two years, or with fine, or with both.
9. See https://chnm.gmu.edu/wwh/p/103.html.
10. Ann Brashares, *The Sisterhood of the Travelling Pants*, 2001.

Chapter 6

1. See https://www.britannica.com/topic/advertising.

2. See Alyque Padamsee, *A Double Life*, 1999, pp. 271–84, for the detailed story about this campaign.
3. *The Medium Is the Massage: An Inventory of Effects* is a book co-created by media analyst Marshall McLuhan and graphic designer Quentin Fiore (1967).

Chapter 7

1. IF AT FIRST YOU DON'T SUCCEED, TRY AGAIN. Don't give up too easily; persistence pays off in the end. The proverb has been traced back to the 'Teacher's Manual' authored by American educator Thomas H. Palmer (1782–1861) and 'The Children of the New Forest' by English novelist Frederick Maryat (1792–1848). It was originally a maxim used to encourage American schoolchildren to do their homework. Palmer wrote in his 'Teacher's Manual': "Tis a lesson you should heed, try, try again. If at first you don't succeed, try, try again.' The saying was popularized by Edward Hickson (1803–1870) in his 'Moral Song' and is now applicable to any kind of activity. From Random House Dictionary of Popular Proverbs and Sayings by Gregory Y. Titelman, 1996, p. 154.

Chapter 8

1. See https://www.theguardian.com/world/1994/may/01/nelsonmandela.southafrica.
2. Audio recording at https://www.openculture.com/2013/01/albert_einstein_expresses_his_admiration_for_mahatma_gandhi.html.
3. See https://www.akanksha.org/.
4. See https://www.teachforindia.org/.
5. See https://www.hindustantimes.com/india-news/meet-the-man-who-fought-to-cap-coronary-stent-price-at-rs-30-000/story-8Nbn7MSAH1NBy17TZjJdUP.html.

Chapter 9

1. 'If any one slew a person—unless it be for murder or for spreading mischief in the land—it would be as if he slew the whole people.'

(Quran 5:32); 'O ye who believe! . . . [do not] kill yourselves, for truly Allah has been to you Most Merciful. If any do that in rancour and injustice, soon shall We cast him into the Fire . . .' (Quran Sura An-Nisa-4:29-30); 'You shall spend in the cause of GOD; do not throw yourselves with your own hands into destruction . . .' (Quran Sura Al-Baqara-2:195).

2. See https://zeenews.india.com/news/nation/ramlila-ground-gets-ready-for-ramdevs-fast_710292.html.

3. See https://timesofindia.indiatimes.com/India/Deoband_first_A_fatwa_against_terror/articleshow/3089161.cms.

4. See https://www.hindustantimes.com/mumbai/need-for-cultural-dialogue-between-india-pak/story-AlaDmB644Idhx97Mgl4z0O.html.

5. Personal communication with Chandrababu Naidu.

6. See https://edition.cnn.com/2009/WORLD/asiapcf/04/17/mumbai.bodies/.

Chapter 10

1. The Bible, 1 Corinthians 11:14.

2. The Bible, Leviticus 20:18.

3. Sahih Muslim, Vol. 5, Book of Drinks, Hadith 5022 23:5022.

4. See https://www.bbc.com/news/world-44209971.

5. See https://www.business-standard.com/article/current-affairs/gurmeet-ram-rahim-singh-verdict-today-details-of-the-14-yr-old-rape-case-117082400529_1.html.

Chapter 11

1. See https://www.britannica.com/topic/Brahman-caste; http://www.dalitweb.org/wp-content/uploads/wp-post-to-pdf-enhanced-cache/1/jathi-varna-and-caste-and-gender-discrimination.pdf.

2. See https://ccnmtl.columbia.edu/projects/mmt/ambedkar/web/readings/aoc_print_2004.pdf.

3. https://www.livemint.com/Leisure/3u2QUPuXBEFPaBQXU2R8mJ/When-will-the-BrahminBania-hegemony-end.

html; https://theprint.in/opinion/brahmins-at-the-top-on-all-indicators-in-states-with-schemes-that-benefit-only-them-study-says/748067/.

4. Act II, Scene II.
5. See https://deathwithdignity.org/.
6. See https://www.medicalnewstoday.com/articles/182951# euthanasia-and-assisted-suicide-.
7. Virginia Berridge, 'Morality and medical science: concepts of narcotic addiction in Britain, 1820–1926', *Annals of Science*, Vol. 36, Issue 1, 1979, pp. 67–85.
8. See https://www.brucekalexander.com/articles-speeches/rat-park/148-addiction-the-view-from-rat-park.
9. See https://www.brucekalexander.com/articles-speeches/rat-park/148-addiction-the-view-from-rat-park.
10. Pascha closed in 2020 due to COVID.
11. See https://wcd.nic.in/act/dowry-prohibition-act-1961.
12. See https://feminisminindia.com/2018/03/12/dowry-related-violence-kills-20-daily/.

Chapter 12

1. See https://www.youtube.com/watch?v=ja6HeLB3kwY.
2. Act I, Scene IV.
3. New York Times THEATER; '"Death and the Maiden" Becomes a Tale of Two Cities', Benedict Nightingale, 10 May 1992.

Chapter 13

1. Donald Hebb, *The Organization of Behaviour*, 1949, p. 62.
2. See https://royalsocietypublishing.org/doi/full/10.1098/rsnr.2017.0034.
3. A.J. Calder, A.D. Lawrence and A.W. Young, 'Neuropsychology of fear and loathing', *Nature Reviews Neuroscience*, 2001.
4. See https://www.ncbi.nlm.nih.gov/pmc/articles/PMC4774859/.
5. Oregon Health & Science University, 'Dopamine conducts prefrontal cortex ensembles: Study reports novel ways that dopamine cells

influence the function of prefrontal cortex of the brain', *ScienceDaily*, 2 April 2019.

6.   Britta K.Hölzel et al., 'Mindfulness practice leads to increases in regional brain gray matter density', *Psychiatry Research: Neuroimaging*, Volume 191, Issue 1, 30 January 2011, pp. 36–43.

7.   https://www.mkgandhi.org/my_religion/36varna_caste.htm. Section on Caste vs Class and his changing views.

Acknowledgements

It's taken years to bring this book to fruition. A huge thanks to Raell, Annie Sequiera and the team at ACE productions for finding old speeches and talks and supporting us from behind. Ida for the cups of tea, coffee, copious amounts of food and for ensuring we had everything we needed at home. Glenda and Yaamini for the courage as we discovered themes and ideas to tease out. Dr Savita Vij for her invaluable assistance with the transcripts. Q, Shazahn and Sharon for the encouragement over the years as well as the brainstorming and suggestions. All of AP's contemporaries, including Gerson Da Cunha, Sabira Merchant and his extended family who spent time discussing parts of this book or AP's legendary personality. Richa and the team at Penguin for the editorial support. My kids, Jai and Zara Poria, for putting up with me through this process. And finally, Cyrus Irani, Caroline Audoir de Valter, Siddharth Chopra and Jill Sheldekar for being amazing sounding boards. Nidhi Bajaj and Manoj Saxena for giving feedback. And, of course, Usha and Raje Saxena for giving me the tools to do what I do, every day.

Scan QR code to access the
Penguin Random House India website